When Jesus Speaks

Will You Listen?

By Ellen Shields

Acknowledgments

I want to thank my Heavenly Father, Jesus my Savior and the Holy Spirit without whom I could not have written this book. Special thanks to John Shields for formatting the manuscript; Elisa Elmshaeuser for her expertise in layout and cover design; Donna Bishop for her beautiful illustrations; Gemma Oyewole for her marvelous job of editing; my beautiful grandchildren who inspire me to pass on my love of God to them; and to my husband, Richard, with whom I love to spend endless hours discussing, discovering, and examining God's Word. What a blessing and encouragement you all are to me.

Scripture quotations from the Holy Bible, English Standard Version® (ESV), copyright© 2001 by Crossway Bibles, a publishing ministry of Good News Publishers. Used by permission. All rights reserved.

Scripture taken from the Holy Bible, New International Version®. Copyright © 1973, 1978, 1984 by International Bible Society. Used by permission of Zondervan. All rights reserved.

All rights reserved. No part of this book may be reproduced or transmitted in any form without prior permission from the author, except for the inclusion of short quotations in a review.

When **Jesus** Speaks, *Will You Listen?*
Copyright © 2019 by Ellen Shields • ellenpshields@gmail.com

❧Dedicated to my father, Ted Metcalf,❧
who taught me from a young age that God is real, that He means what He says, and He keeps every promise He has ever made.

Table of Contents

Lesson 1	Introduction: *Jesus Speaks*	1
Lesson 2	Humility: *Lessons From a Child*	13
Lesson 3	Faith – Part 1: *Lessons Learned While on a Walk with Jesus*	27
Lesson 4	Faith – Part 2: *Lessons From Our Early Brothers and Sisters*	39
Lesson 5	Holy Spirit: *Jesus Teaches the Role of the Holy Spirit in Our Lives*	49
Lesson 6	Becoming a Servant: *Jesus Washes the Apostles' Feet*	63
Lesson 7	Hypocrisy: *A Lesson from the Sermon on the Mount*	75
Lesson 8	Prayer – Part 1: *Jesus Teaches His Followers to Pray*	87
Lesson 9	Prayer – Part 2: *Parable of the Persistent Friend*	101
Lesson 10	Anger: *A Lesson from the Sermon on the Mount*	117
Lesson 11	Worry: *Lessons from the Flowers and Birds*	127
Lesson 12	Forgiveness – Part 1: *Lessons from an Unmerciful Servant*	139
Lesson 13	Forgiveness – Part 2: *More Lessons from the Unmerciful Servant*	149

When Jesus taught, He did not use pressure tactics, nor did He strongarm His audience; He spoke... He waited... and then He walked away, leaving His words for His listeners to ponder. He didn't use gimmicks, and never put on a really big show featuring THE One and Only Joe Blow from Palestine who speaks for the biggest synagogue this side of the Jordan River! No, when Jesus spoke, His listeners were left to choose how they would react to the information.

Today, we have the same challenge when we hear the words of Jesus. Some listeners will immediately believe them and want to hear more. While others will be skeptical as they contemplate what changes it might mean to the lifestyle they have come to love.

The words Jesus spoke back in His day, and that He speaks to us today, are meant to be life-changing. He intends for us to take them seriously and to apply them to our everyday lives. Each one of us must choose to either believe and obey the words of Jesus or to ignore them and turn away. It is our choice.

A phrase I noticed Jesus used often in the New Testament is "I tell you the truth." I began to underline them in my Bible: 78 times He used the term, "I tell you the truth," and 72 times He said, "I tell you." It dawned on me that Jesus used these phrases purposely to catch the attention of his audience. Today we might use the phrases, "Listen up" or "Don't miss this point!" The phrase is used in order to cause the listener to pay special attention to what the teacher is about to teach. As I thought about that, the idea for this book was born.

We know every word Jesus spoke was important, but at times He did stress and emphasize certain concepts to His audience. In this study we are going to look at 12 different lessons Jesus taught using the phrase, "I tell you the truth." I want you to take each lesson personally, as if Jesus were speaking directly to you (because, actually, He is). Now, picture yourself on a beautiful sunny day out on a grassy meadow surrounded by a group of friends when all of a sudden Jesus walks up and sits down with you! Everyone is crazy with excitement waiting to hear what the master teacher has to say. I can just imagine hearing the voice of Jesus as He begins, "Girls, I tell you the truth..."

Ellen

Introduction — Lesson One

"All Scripture is breathed out by God and profitable for teaching, for reproof, for correction, and for training in righteousness, that the man of God may be competent, equipped for every good work." –2 Timothy 3:16-17

I am so excited you have chosen to study with me. My prayer as I write these lessons is that my heart, and yours too, will be completely open to the words of Jesus. Our Lord has so much to tell us, but He needs us to listen. When Jesus spoke to the masses, some listened intently, and others were skeptical to say the least. Each person listened for their own reasons; some just to learn where the next handout would be. Others couldn't wait to report the words of Jesus to their rabbis in hopes of stirring up trouble for Him. But then, there were those who listened because they were amazed at His teachings and they believed Jesus to be who He claimed to be: their long-awaited Messiah.

Unfortunately, things have not changed so much in these past 2,000 years. We too, listen to Jesus for various reasons. Some just want to have a blessed life, but are unwilling to make a total commitment. Others love God as long as things go their way, but at the first sign of difficulties, they're outta there! Then there are those who genuinely love God and want more than anything in the whole world to please Him. They follow Him through good times and bad. I know this describes you!

Jesus taught His disciples so much in the three short years of His ministry on earth. Many things He said are written down for us, but as John said, "Were every one of them to be written , I suppose that the world itself could not contain the books that would be written" (John 21:25). As Jesus went along and taught day after day, one can tell that some things He said were more accentuated by Him than others. These passages are borne out by the words, "I tell you the truth" and "I tell you." I believe when He spoke these phrases He was putting an extra emphasis on the subject at hand. It always reminds me of the old commercials that said, "When EF Hutton speaks . . ." followed by a hush throughout the busy room. When Jesus says, "I tell you the truth," it is a announcement that He is about to say something to which we all must pay special attention.

In this study we will examine nine such topics that relate to our lives directly. These topics are not all easy to listen to. Some will demand a change in our behavior or attitude. You and I will have a lot of choices to make during the coming weeks. Will we listen to Jesus and obey Him? Or will we stubbornly or passively refuse to obey?

In today's lesson we are going to look briefly at each lesson topic in this study. This is meant to give you an overview of the lessons to come. So whip out your Swords, sharpen your pencils, and let's begin to listen to Jesus as He tells us the truth !

⊱Humility⊰

☕ **READ: Matthew 18:1-4**

One of the most unbelievable questions ever posed to Jesus was from his disciples concerning a debate they had going with each other.

1. What question did the disciples ask Jesus? *Matthew 18:1*

2. Jesus said they must change and become like what? *Matthew 18:3*

Our society today would have us believe that humility is a weak, nasty character flaw. The world believes that without self promotion one can't get ahead in this world. Humility is seen as a weakness in a person, not a virtue. It is human nature to think like this. Even Christians can believe it. Jesus' disciples sure did. That's why Jesus said, "Unless you change, you won't be able to enter the kingdom of heaven."

Having a humble spirit takes work on our part. First, it takes a genuine desire in our heart to want to be humble. Then it takes lots of prayer and determination.

3. What does Jesus say will happen if one is not humble? *Matthew 18:3*

⊱Faith⊰

☕ **READ: Mark 11:20-23**

4. According to the Hebrew writer, what is faith? *Hebrews 11:6*

The wonder of faith is that one believes in something that cannot be seen. We believe in God, in Jesus, in the Holy Spirit and in heaven even though they are not physically visible. Faith is not faith if one can see the answer. It doesn't take faith to believe the meteorologist when he says it will rain tomorrow when we look outside and it is cloudy and cold. But what if you are Noah and the weather man tells you it's going to rain? Now we're talking faith girlfriend. To believe God when He gives us a promise, even when we have no rain clouds to back it up, now that is faith.

5. What does Jesus say a person of faith can do if they do not doubt? *Mark 11:23*

Genuine faith, believes in the promises of God—all of them. And believes them without the slightest doubt. Noah surely believed God when He said it was going to rain, though he had never seen it rain a day in his entire life! Do you have faith like that? A faith that would never doubt God's judgment or His ability, or His promises?

When God told Adam and Eve to run around and enjoy their lovely life in the Garden of Eden but to not eat from one tree, He meant it. However, when Eve saw that beautiful fruit, she felt its roundness, and smelled its enticing aroma . . . it was lovely in every way. Her senses got the best of her, and she threw God's promises out the window, well, the garden then.

What is it about us that we think we know better than God? That we can decide when the time is right to have our way. That it is our decision as to who lives or who dies. Faith is believing in our unseen Father, His power to do the impossible, and His knowledge to know what is best in all aspects of our life.

6. Who is your faith hero from the Bible, and why?

Jesus' response to the apostles when they were terrified of dying while in the middle of a frightening storm out on the Sea of Galilee seems remarkable to me at times. Fear of imminent death seems a reasonable reaction to most of us. But, look at the response of Jesus.

7. What did Jesus say in rebuke to the disciples' fear of dying? *Mark 4:40*

Faith that cannot weather a storm or trial is not faith at all. Jesus had no tolerance for those men who lost their trust in Him when things got stormy. God expects us to trust in Him, in His promises, and in His ability to accomplish things in His proper time. It makes no difference whether things are going smoothly or we are experiencing the most difficult trial of our life. We must not expect God to always make our way comfortable. Nor should we immediately conclude God has abandoned us, and that He doesn't care about us when He tells us no. We must always give God room to do what

He knows is the right thing to do, even when it conflicts with the deepest desire of our hearts.

∽ Holy Spirit ∽

READ: John 16:7-14

The subject of the Holy Spirit can be downright mysterious at times. Many believers go through life and never fully understand His function in the church and in their hearts. After the Last Supper in the upper room, Jesus told the apostles that He was going to have to leave them. They were so disappointed and full of grief that He could not tell them much more. But He did tell them not to worry; life would be alright because He was going to send them a Counselor who would take His place. This Counselor is the Holy Spirit.

Up to this point in time, the Holy Spirit had worked through a few individuals to carry out God's work.

> **8. The Holy Spirit is first mentioned in Genesis 1:2. What do we find Him doing?**

The Spirit has never stopped working since time began. However, His role has changed tremendously since the Day of Pentecost when He entered man's heart.

The Holy Spirit is mentioned in every book in the New Testament, except 2nd and 3rd John. He has become a very active force in every believer's life.

> **9. How does one receive the Holy Spirit?** *Acts 2:38*
>
> **10. What do we find the Spirit doing for believers in the New Testament?**
>
> *John 16:8*
>
> *Galatians 5:22-23*

The Spirit has a very difficult task to accomplish. He is working in the hearts of unbelievers trying to get them to acknowledge the sin in their lives. And He is living inside the heart of each believer giving us what we need to overcome our sins and trials. He is actively giving us wisdom and answers to our problems and dilemmas. He gives us inexplicable comfort during excruciating trials, approaching the Father on our behalf when our hearts are too laden with grief or guilt to speak on our own. The Holy Spirit is one of the greatest gifts our Heavenly Father gives His sons and daughters.

⁂ Become a Servant ⁂

READ: John 13:1-17

You and I can take great comfort in seeing the transformation the apostles made as they worked and walked alongside Jesus during His ministry years. As Jesus taught and preached, His disciples digested each word according to their own understanding and opinions. Many times they drew the wrong conclusion to His lessons. And never more so than when Jesus explained the importance of being a servant.

Instead of observing and learning from the humble actions of Jesus, they preferred to look into the future and see themselves risen to a grandiose status with assignments fit for a King's right hand man. Because of this attitude these men had become virtually useless to Jesus. So, during the last meal that Jesus would observe with His apostles, He taught them a lesson on becoming a servant that would change them forever.

11. What were the apostles arguing about on the night of the Passover? *Luke 22:24-27*

The same night, as the apostles argued among themselves, Judas was still pondering whether or not to betray Jesus. What a heavy burden for Jesus as He mentally prepared Himself for His crucifixion.

12. Explain what Jesus did in response to this discussion and the action of Judas. *John 13:3-5*

13. What did Jesus expect the apostles to learn from this experience? What should you and I learn? *John 13:15-17*

Washing the feet of others is translated into serving others even if it means doing something we are uncomfortable doing, or despise doing, or worst of all, think is beneath us.

⊱Hypocrisy⊰

READ: Matthew 6:2-8

Jesus did a lot of teaching on the subject of hypocrisy. But those listening didn't always grasp His full meaning. He seemed to get them to understand the fundamentals of doing things that they were commanded to do, but they did not follow His meaning when He told them to do these things for the glory of God. In fact, quite the opposite was true. They were brought up and taught all their lives that one should toot his own horn at each and every opportunity.

14. What did Jesus warn His followers not to do in Matthew 6:1?

The specific acts of kindness or righteousness are never described by Jesus because they do not matter. *Why* one is doing what they are doing is what matters. It all comes down to one's heart.

15. Name some righteous acts we do every day that we might be tempted to boast about or do for show.

It is so easy to fall into the mindset of our first century brothers and sisters and do things for the accolades we gain from others. As Jesus explains, it is very possible to do the right thing for the wrong reason.

16. What does Jesus say about those who toot their own horn? *Matthew 6:2*

17. How secretive are we to be in regards to our giving? *Matthew 6:3*

18. What is hypocritical about letting other women know I gave $300.00 for the Ladies Retreat Campership Fund?

19. What is the dreadful fate of those of us who are hypocritical? *Matthew 23:27, 33*

Everything we do under public eye has the potential to bring glory, honor, and praise to God or kudos f ourselves. When we give, when we pray, when we do kind things for others, God is honored. When we seek credit and a pat on the back, we are no longer pleasing to God, but have become a hypocrite and are a disgrace. Likewise, when we judge someone while ignoring our own shortcomings, we step right up to the level of hypocrites. Something we must continue to ask ourselves is: Whose reward am I seeking?

❧Prayer❧

 READ: Luke 11:1-13

Does God always answer your prayers with a resounding yes? If your answer is no, what goes through your mind as you ponder why He said no? Have you ever doubted God heard you? Or thought He is too busy helping others more important than you? Or that your problems are too insignificant and are of no importance to Him? I'm sure it would be easy to come up with a list of reasons why we believe God did not hear us, or sadly, we might even think that He just doesn't care.

Prayer is one of the most valuable blessings a believer possesses. Our ancient brothers and sisters in the Old Testament did not have the same privilege of communicating with the Father as those of us living after Jesus' death. In the Old Testament, one had to speak to God through judges, priests and prophets. But Jesus changed all of that when He was sacrificed on the cross for us. Now we have open and complete access to God anytime our hearts desire to speak to Him.

One would think that speaking to the Creator of the Universe would be the highlight of our day, the highest honor and most treasured gift known to man. And it truly is, but we have so taken it for granted that it has lost its uniqueness and hardly feels like a privilege at all. It has become rather humdrum at times. Sometimes we pray out of habit or with crossed fingers just in case it works, not believing or expecting God will care, listen or do what we are asking.

A key element to having a super strong prayer life, one that can move mountains, is having a close relationship with God. And in order to have a real relationship, one must desire above all else to know God, obey Him and please Him. One cannot fake a relationship with God; He can spot that a mile away, so to speak.

20. What does Peter say determines whether or not our prayers are heard? *1 Peter 3:12*

21. Paul says we can know God's will if we do what? *Romans 12:2*

When Jesus Speaks, Will You Listen?

22. What do Jesus and John say one must do in order to have their prayers answered?

John 15:16-17

1 John 3:22

Jesus gave His disciples and all believers the most beautiful prayer as a model. In it we learn how to relate to God and what to talk to Him about. But there is a very big prerequisite one must be aware of if their prayers are going to be answered yes, and if their mountains are going to move.

23. What two things does Jesus say one must have or not have in order to move those troublesome mountains? *Mark 11:22-24*

24. How does the Holy Spirit help us in our prayer life? *Romans 8:26*

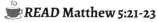

❧ Anger ❧

READ Matthew 5:21-23

It is amazing to me how much Jesus had to say about anger. In speaking to a huge crowd one day while sitting on the hillside, Jesus began teaching things they had never heard from any rabbi before. The Jewish religious leaders in the time of Jesus were experts at finding loopholes in the Law. They had jars and jars of scrolls describing in detail how one could get around the Law. So when Jesus taught that their behavior, attitudes, and motives were more important than following the letter of the law; His audience was left baffled to say the least.

25. Read these two passages. What is the law concerning murder? What does Jesus teach concerning murder?

Exodus 20:13

Matthew 5:21-22

The Jewish punishment for murder was a death sentence ordered by the civil magistrate. Jesus said that God's punishment for being angry was eternal damnation in hell. Just try to sugarcoat that! The death sentence of the courts was a cakewalk compared to God's punishment for being angry.

26. What does Paul teach about anger? *Ephesians 4:26-27*

27. What are some sins one commits while angry?

28. What is the punishment for those who sin in their anger? *Matthew 5:22*

Jesus is not speaking of the momentary bursts of frustration that we feel when the hangers get tangled, or the kids spill red Kool-Aid on the carpet, or the new puppy wets on the couch. But rather what we *do* when we are frustrated or angry. Do we just say "Ugh!"? Or do we scream obscenities at the hangers, hit or belittle the children, or kick the puppy across the room? What we do while we are angry is what is being judged.

The anger that is like murder is our unrighteous anger – anger we feel because our pride has been injured, things did not go our way, or someone made work for us and we feel put out. The outburst of anger and getting revenge is what Jesus is talking about.

Being angry and sinning is a very serious offense to God. He does not look on it lightly. There is no wink wink, or "that's okay Sweetie." We must be very honest with ourselves and see our problem as God sees it. Sinning while angry is a deal breaker as far as God is concerned.

❧ Worry ❧

READ Luke 12:22-31

Have you ever tried not to worry about something? It can be a very difficult thing to do, especially when going through a trial or crisis. Jesus, knowing human nature, took an opportunity to teach a very straightforward lesson on the subject. He doesn't leave any leeway for extenuating circumstances, or just this once since this situation is so bad. No, He sums it all up and just says simply, "Don't do it!" I think sometimes I'd like to take Him to task over some instances in my life . . . until I think of His life. Okay, I'll be quiet and listen.

> **29. What kinds of things did Jesus say not to worry over?** *Luke 12:22*
>
> **30. What do you tend to worry about?**
>
> **31. What point is Jesus making in Luke 12:23?**

If God can create this world, hold back the waves of the sea, and send out the thunder and lightning, don't you suppose He can take care of you? If you are nodding your head yes, while ringing your hands at the same time, something is wrong. And most likely girlfriend, you have a trust issue. If the birds are taken care of by God when they don't do a single solitary thing, then you, God's valuable daughter, will be taken care of all the more! We must believe that fact to our core, and then act on it. Like my dad used to say, "To die and go to heaven is not the worst thing that can happen to a Christian!" It takes tremendous faith in God and in His promises for one to conquer worry. But I promise you, if Jesus says we can do it, then it can be done.

> **32. What did Jesus call those who worried?** *Luke 12:28*

Jesus knew how difficult life could be. He knew the struggles people were going through and yet He still berated them for worrying. Today, you and I have modern kinds of problems one might point out. But take away the new-fangled gizmos and high-tech devices, change the outfits, and you'll find we all worry about the same things: food, shelter, and the future. Jesus calls worry a waste of time that can't change a thing. Then He reminds us that God already knows about our problems anyway!

33. What is one to spend time thinking about instead of worry? *Luke 12:31*

God is a loving God, truly He is. He is stronger than the strongest, wiser than the wisest, and He cares for you. All we have to do is believe it, obey and then bask in the blessings that come from that trust. Short and simply put: worry is physical evidence that one does not truly trust God. On the other hand, peace in adversity and calm in a trial is evidence one has put their faith in God. When it comes to our troubles Jesus said, "Do not worry about them."

❧Forgiveness❧

READ: Matthew 18:21-35

Would you agree with me that it is very difficult to forgive someone when they purposely harm you? Peter must have had a case like that in mind when he asked Jesus if forgiving others seven times was enough. Aren't you glad it was Peter who asked that question and not you! We can learn a lot from Peter's question and from Jesus' answer.

In the preceding verses we learn that it is our responsibility to do everything in our power to reconcile with those who have wronged us. Peter has some reservations about that and is astonished at the answer Jesus gives.

34. Why do you believe it is difficult to forgive others when they have wronged or hurt you?

35. What is the response of the apostles when Jesus told them to forgive seven times a day if necessary? *Luke 17:3-5*

36. Why do we forgive others? *Matthew 6:14-15*

When Jesus Speaks, Will You Listen?

37. Make a list of blessings that come to the one who forgives. Now make a list of the blessings that come to the one who is forgiven.

Blessings to the Forgiver	*Blessings to the Forgiven*

38. Paul tells us that all Scripture is breathed out by God. Name four ways one can profit by reading and applying God's Word.

1.

2.

3.

4.

What a marvelous spiritual journey you and I are about to embark on together. I just love to see Scripture come alive in my mind. To look deeply into subjects that Jesus chose to stress to His beloved followers just makes my heart want to burst with excitement and anticipation. It also makes me wonder how I would have reacted had I been there to hear Jesus with my own ears. To know these truths we are about to study are near and dear to our Lord's heart, and to know how vital they are concerning our eternity, will make us want to sit up and take notice, take notes and muster a determination to be like the receptive sisters who followed after Jesus. The sister who listened intently as Jesus *told her the truth*.

❧ Humility ❧ Lesson Two

"I tell you the truth, unless you change and become like little children you will never enter the kingdom of heaven ... Therefore, whoever humbles himself like this child is the greatest ..." –Matthew 18:3-4

In his book, "Mere Christianity," C.S. Lewis said, "True humility is not thinking less of yourself; it is thinking of yourself less." It was once said that the instant a man thinks he has humility he loses it! Humility is a funny thing, it is easily faked, easy to mistakenly think one has, and easily dismissed as nonessential if it is greatness one is seeking. It is a virtue the world does not value – nor do any "greatness" seeking folks.

But humility means everything to God. It is a subject that ribbons throughout the entire Bible. If you are a daily Bible reader, you are aware how often the subject comes up. It is addressed in nearly every book of the Bible. It is what God has looked for in man's heart since the creation of the world. Let's take a few moments and look at a few passages that will reveal how very important it is to our Father that we, His daughters, strive to be humble.

1. How does God feel about those who are not humble?

Psalm 18:27

Psalm 147:6

Proverbs 6:16-17

What is first in the list of things God hates?

2. What does God expect the humble to do?

Micah 6:8

James 3:13

When Jesus Speaks, Will You Listen?

3. What will God do for the humble?

   Psalm 25:9

   Proverbs 3:34

   Isaiah 66:2

   Matthew 23:12 & James 4:10

God is always pleased with those who show humility in their lives—and He always despises pride and haughtiness. I think it is sad that after the world was created, it only took six chapters (Genesis 6) before God had to destroy all of mankind (with the exception of the Noah family) for their wickedness and pride. Humility has always been, and will always be, a struggle for us humans.

With these thoughts in mind, let's join Jesus and his disciples in Capernaum. The disciples have come to Jesus and asked a very telling question. Knowing their hearts and their thoughts Jesus teaches a much needed lesson on humility.

Notice how Jesus challenges His followers to pause and look honestly into their hearts in order to learn the genuine meaning of humility. This lesson was not an easy lesson for His followers to accept because they thought of humility as a bad word denoting weakness and unworthiness. Some of us are going to find ourselves thinking the same thing. Humility goes against human nature; it is not an innate or natural trait. No one is born humble. It must be taught, observed, practiced, and sought after. If we are serious in our desire to be humble, we will have to work hard and examine our hearts to make it happen. It will most likely mean making some changes in our attitude, motives, and in the way we look at others.

READ: Matthew 18:1-6

4. What question did the disciples ask Jesus? *Matthew 18:1*

5. What kingdom do you suppose the disciples were thinking of?

What a question to ask the Lord! The fact that they had the arrogance to ask such a question illustrates they didn't have a clue what greatness was in the eyes of God. It also highlights their lack of awareness of the grave consequences awaiting those who seek worldly greatness for themselves. To the apostles greatness was power, position, and prestige. They all thought of themselves as Jesus' elite and just knew Jesus would have special positions for them in His new kingdom. Andrew was the first apostle to meet Jesus. Peter had been given the keys to the kingdom. John was the apostle whom Jesus loved. James not only was a brother to the famous John, but was also a cousin of Jesus. If we were to look closely at each apostle, we would find men following Jesus in hopes of being someone special in the new Kingdom Jesus so often talked about.

It must have pained Jesus to see His disciples seeking personal greatness knowing they could never become the leaders He needed them to be unless they changed their ambitions. The disciples were following their own personal dreams, completely oblivious of their lack of humility.

The disciples had a huge obstacle to overcome. Pride and vanity can be obstacles for us to overcome as well. If the new church was to survive and flourish after Jesus was gone, His followers had to see their role in the kingdom in a completely different light.

In the eyes of our God, true greatness is determined by a man's humility. It has nothing to do with one's deeds, prominence, power, money, education or popularity. God measures our greatness by how humbly we live our lives. "Not by the great things we achieve?" you ask. No, but rather by how humble we are. Truly the least important person in God's eyes is the one who seeks greatness in His kingdom.

As Jesus listens to His disciples' question, He answers with a very unexpected lesson on humility. Jesus uses hyperbole in answer to their question to emphasize the major change that needs to take place in their attitudes and in their hearts.

READ: Matthew 18:2

> **6. Whom did Jesus call to become His visual aid?**

Jesus is just about to answer the question, "Who is the greatest?" Let's pause here and look at the situation for a moment from the eyes of those present that day. Jesus is doing the teaching. His listeners include His apostles, His disciples, their children, and servants of the house. They are in the area where the apostle Peter now lived, and possibly Peter's home. The children would be staying out of the adults' way, not paying much attention to the adult discussion until the subject of who's the greatest came up. This question seems to have struck a nerve with Jesus. In answer to their question, Jesus called a child to himself. After the shock of Jesus putting a child in the limelight, His followers must have thought to themselves, "Come on, Jesus, stop kidding around. Send that kid away and tell us who is the greatest."

Children were the least prestigious living in a household. In the time of Jesus, children were looked upon as insignificant and unimportant. They had absolutely no social status in the pecking order of life. As far as greatness goes, you could not get any lower.

What Jesus was about to explain would shatter the apostles' personal dreams of grandeur in the new kingdom, and at the same time force them to search their hearts as they thought about what their

When Jesus Speaks, Will You Listen?

role *would be* in this new kingdom Jesus talked about.

READ: Matthew 18:3

> 7. What two adjustments did Jesus say His followers had to make in order to be great in the kingdom of heaven?
>
> 8. What change did the disciples need to make?
>
> 9. How do you think the disciples expected Jesus to answer their question?

"You must become like this child," was definitely not the answer the disciples were expecting. Surely Jesus didn't really expect them to become like this little child! They must have thought, "Jesus be serious. We have worked alongside you for three years. What could we possibly have in common with this insignificant child."

Did Jesus really expect His apostles to stop thinking about self promotions and which of them He would choose for the highest position in the kingdom? YES, He did! Jesus expected them to give it all up. But these men were pretty bent on having their special leadership roles.

It's easy for us to be critical of the followers of Jesus. Their lack of judgment, understanding and foresight might even make you want to smile a bit. But the truth is, we can and do have the same sense of arrogance and pride in our own hearts at times. Of course we know better than to be so outspoken and open about it, but, oh how we have our clever, subtle ways of getting others to see how absolutely fabulous we are. Who among us would post a picture on Facebook of ourselves losing or falling short of a task? Normally, our posts depict only the best of our lives . . . I'm just sayin'.

Let's think about some ways that we can fall into the same temptation of thinking more highly of ourselves than we ought.

> 10. List ways one can seek power and status in the church today.
>
> 11. What does one need to change in order to be like a child?

The apostles had so bought into the world's definition of humility that they couldn't see that their Self-centeredness could cause them to neglect others. In order to get them to see the seriousness of the matter, Jesus made a powerful point by comparing His followers to a child.

This passage points out clearly what the disciples thought of themselves. Their question did not have anything to do with how to get into the kingdom, or even if they would be part of the kingdom. They assumed that would happen. What they wanted to know was, among those of them in the room, which one was the greatest? The notion that this might not be a legitimate question never entered their minds.

12. What did Jesus say would happen to those who did not change?

13. What is the full long-range implication of this statement?

To the astonishment of everyone, Jesus changed the focus of their question from who's the greatest in the kingdom, to who will enter the kingdom at all.

I believe Jesus had their full attention now. Our heroic brothers who thought themselves so very important were in a precarious and most embarrassing situation. They now stand humiliated, with their souls in jeopardy for asking such a question.

I'm sure the men in the room took to the word "change" much like you and I might. But to add to it such drastic and eternal consequences had to be hard to hear. Not only were these followers' dreams of power and honor shot down, but they might not make it into the kingdom at all! How could that be? Oh my, everyone in the room is on the edge of their cushions now!

As the disciples stared at the child standing beside Jesus, dozens of questions must have run through their minds. The one thing the apostles thought that they had going for them was how vitally important they were to Jesus and His kingdom. Now Jesus is telling them that if they didn't change, they were in danger of eternal damnation. Once again, no matter how hard you try, you cannot sugarcoat that statement. Their prideful feeling of superiority had to change.

Though this statement shocked the disciples, it was not the first lesson Jesus had taught on the importance of having a humble heart. It also was not the first lesson He had taught on how to enter the kingdom of heaven. But the apostles never seemed to have put the two together. Let's stop again for a moment and look at a few Scriptures that point out various factors that will keep one from entering the kingdom of heaven.

14. According to these passages, what does one have to do to enter the kingdom of heaven?

   Matthew 5:19-20

   Matthew 7:21-22

   John 3:5

Wow! When we compare humility to eternal life, it doesn't take long to understand the deep importance Jesus is placing on humility. Lack of humility brings the same punishment as unrighteousness, discarding the will of God, or ignoring baptism. Not entering the kingdom of heaven is a heavy punishment for having a prideful and arrogant heart. Yet, that's exactly what Jesus warned His followers in Capernaum would happen if they didn't change. This should make us all stop and take pause and honestly examine our hearts for any signs of pride or ego.

READ: Matthew 18:4

Here in verse 4 is where Jesus gets down to the nitty gritty and answers the disciples' question of which one of them was the greatest.

15. In what way is a child humble? What aspect of a child's humility do adults need to emulate?

Wouldn't you love to have seen the faces of the children in the room that day? They were probably laughing and snickering at their friend standing at Jesus' side. But the adults in the room were not amused. They were bewildered and confused, wondering how and why they were supposed to humble themselves and become like this little child. It just did not make sense.

16. Why is it so difficult to humble ourselves and serve others?

There is something very pure and honest about the humility of children. It is no wonder Jesus chose a child as his example. Though we can all attest to the fact children are not always humble by nature, yet, they do share some humbling qualities: they accept their status as children, they know who is in control and it's OK, and they trust authority without question. They can change activities easily when told they must. They never have dreams or aspirations of taking control. Even the strongest willed child doesn't want control, though he or she fights for it tooth-and-nail. Children are happy to sit and play in the back seat of a car on a long trip. They don't expect to drive, map out their destination, or to finance the trip.

This is the humility Jesus is talking about. Accepting our place in the kingdom without dreams of power or prestige; trusting God to control and direct every aspect of our lives. That is what Jesus wanted His followers to understand. He wanted them to see themselves as they really were: lowly servants of each other. He wanted them to find fulfillment in ministering to others, encouraging and meeting the needs of others, not their own! Jesus demonstrated the highest form of humility when He left heaven for our sake.

17. How does Paul describe the humility of Jesus in Philippians 2:8?

Jesus' life is a living example of humility in its purest form. Think about it, He left the comforts of heaven in order to serve others! If Jesus could lower Himself for us, shouldn't we be able to put our pride and ego aside and seek the well-being of others?

18. Who is the greatest Christian you know and why are they the greatest?

19. Make a list of qualities in a person that the world deems great, then another list of qualities in a person that God deems great.

World	God

Our society teaches us to be strong, powerful individuals who climb to the top of our field whatever the cost. To help our children get ahead, we instill this at a very young age. We have t-ball, beginning

When Jesus Speaks, Will You Listen?

swimming, gymnastics, dance, and music lessons. We even have Baby Einstein programs. Name any academic achievement, sport, or art, and you'll find classes for your babies to attend. We, like our brothers and sisters in Jesus' day, are taught humility is a weakness and we must find ways to one-up-one another. We are influenced, taught, and pressured by the world to be self-promoting. To look at life any other way is not easy, nor is it natural.

Martin Luther is quoted, "Oh, do not think to be great, but to be little. Becoming great will come of itself if you have become little." But how does one become little? Let's look at some practical ways in which we can measure humility in our everyday lives. Humility can only be learned. Though it may come more easily for some, it is not natural for anyone. We all must fight the instinct to want our own way to some degree or another. Our brother Paul was a very humble man, but not from the beginning.

Let's look at some practical ways he taught the early Christians to exercise their humility.

20. What do these Scriptures tell us about humility and dealing with others?

Romans 12:16

Philippians 2:3

READ: Matthew 18:5

Jesus once again redirects the focus of His lesson. This time He directs His attention away from the child at his side and back to the listeners in the room.

Now that Jesus had answered their question, He began to make an application. To begin, His thoughts turned to those who would humble themselves and accept that childlike status: being willing to put others first and giving up all dreams of self-importance and prestige.

21. Who is the little child that Jesus is referring to in verse 5?

The word for child in Greek is *paidion*. It can mean either a young child or a beginner of something. Jesus has referred to both definitions in this passage. He started out speaking of young children and how His disciples needed to become like them in their humility. But now He switches the meaning and is referring to the little child as the believers who are both young in their faith and humble. He was still pointing to the visual aid at His side when He said, "a little child like this," but He was referring to a beginner believer who was humble and vulnerable.

The apostles thought so highly of themselves that they actually felt a notch above other followers of Jesus, especially new followers, or quiet shy followers, or extra kindhearted and compassionate followers. If forced to think about it, the apostles might have felt obligated to be kind, hospitable, or encouraging to a fellow brother in the faith, but they did not by any means feel that that person was as good or important as they were. Being humble was a sign of weakness to them, and the truth is they truly felt they were superior to others, even amongst themselves! This self-assessment would never get them the power and recognition they longed for and felt they deserved.

We can feel the same way at times, displaying false humility and patronizing our brothers and sisters while pretending to care about them. This is not the humility Jesus is talking about. "Welcoming a little child like this," isn't simply displaying hospitality toward others, but rather accepting others as valuable and important; seeing their humility as an attribute, not a chink in their armor; and not using their humility as a way to take advantage of them. The world sees humility as weakness which makes the humble person rather worthless and insignificant in their eyes. We believers must fight the temptation to think the same way.

22. **Name ways we can welcome little children or humble believers in the church.**

23. **Look over the following situations and note how those who are proud would react and how those who are humble would react. Then decide which way you, on a good day, would most likely react to each scenario.**

   a. A teacher is needed at church for a class that is notoriously difficult to teach.

   b. Someone is needed to do a non-limelight job (cleaning, organizing, giving rides to the elderly or children, cleaning the building, etc.).

   c. A suggestion by an enthusiastic newcomer is brought up, but you don't like it.

   d. A new Christian wants to lead a ministry, but you know you would do a better job.

The way we react in these types of situations is exactly what Jesus means by "welcoming a little child like this." We must get over ourselves and look out for the interest of others. And when we do, not only is Jesus glorified, but a magnificent transformation takes place in our hearts.

The phrase "in His name" can mean because of me, or for my sake, or even just because he is one of My disciples. I believe Jesus is speaking of all three definitions in this passage. Each time we put our own ambitions aside and receive and encourage a humble brother or sister, we are in reality receiving and serving Jesus! That can be either a thrilling or chilling thought.

But how does this play out in our everyday life? And if this kind of humility does not come naturally to us, how do we acquire it? Good questions, let's dig a little deeper.

24. How do we receive someone in the name of, for the sake of, or because of Jesus?

25. What personality types would have the most trouble with humility in the church today? Why would they?

26. What is the temptation for bold, extrovert type personalities in the church?

27. For which personality type is humility easiest?

28. Which type are you? What particular areas of humility are the hardest for you to control?

It is so easy to be swayed by confident, aggressive, and assertive people. We might even admire them. They can bulldoze their way past the quieter, humble person. It is the way of life. The weaker step aside for the stronger. But Jesus tears this theory to shreds. He really means for the strong, both in the faith and in personality, to back off, keep their aspirations in check, and watch out for the other guy, the underdog, the shy unassertive types, and those who are new or weak in the faith. Jesus always aligns Himself with the humble when they are being mistreated by the assertive.

Sadly, the world does not applaud acts of humility—but God does. He considers the humble person great in the kingdom. The kingdom is made up of humble saints. You'll not find proud, conceited people in the kingdom of heaven. And we don't have to plant a hundred churches, preach to thousands, or make millions of dollars in order to be a spiritual giant in the eyes of our heavenly Father. A spiritual giant is one who puts others first, who seeks the welfare of others because of a genuine concern for them. Jesus told our brothers and sisters in Capernaum that when they accepted someone weaker than themselves, they were accepting Him. Doesn't that just warm your heart?

**READ: Matthew 25:34-40**

29. Note the situations in which Jesus saw others serving Him.

30. Name 3 ways we can do something for Jesus as we are doing things for each other.

31. To whom did Jesus say we should do these acts of kindness? Verse 40

That, dear sister, is how we should receive everyone we know, as if they and their ideas, are Jesus'. If Jesus came to our work party at church, we'd trip all over ourselves to support the ministry. We'd first of all show up. Then we'd allow Him to make all the decisions, giving way to all our fabulous ideas. Why, we'd even let Him choose the color of the paint without a fuss. This is the same attitude we should have with each other.

Jesus said that when we welcome and receive each other, it is the same as receiving Him. We must love others to the extent that we can see their needs and put these needs before our desires to be noticed, praised, and patted on the back. If that means not having our way in exchange for someone else being encouraged or built up, then so be it. And if someone else gets the glory and praise for a job you could have done better; well, I believe Jesus would say, "Way to go, girl! I'm proud of you!" Humility is worth working at—the rewards are heavenly.

READ: Matthew 18:6

In verse 6 Jesus explains the importance of humility by describing very graphically the fate of those who will not change and become humble. When we refuse to act humbly, our haughty and selfish attitude becomes the instrument used to cause others to lose their faith or sin. We have all seen this happen in the church; a self-centered brother or sister hurts and discourages someone, causing him to leave the church and turn away from God. Causing one to lose his or her soul comes with a very heavy penalty.

The little ones in this verse are Jesus' followers who possess this childlike humility. They are Christians who are susceptible to pressure, too shy to speak up, easily ignored, those on the periphery of our fellowship. Their humility has made them vulnerable and they either will not stand up for themselves or they cannot. Either way, it is our fault if we trip them up. But how do we do that? Again, Paul sheds some light on the practical side of this subject. It takes a huge amount of spiritual growth and humility to do what Paul is about to tell us.

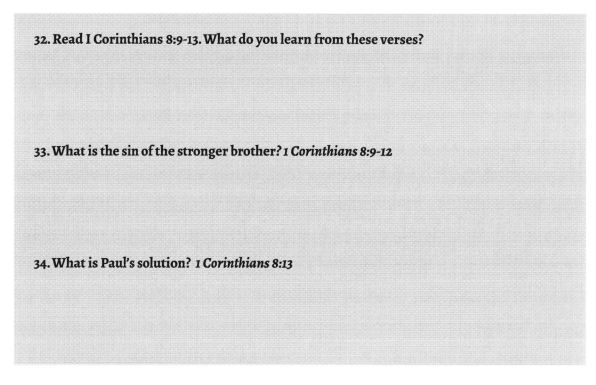

32. Read I Corinthians 8:9-13. What do you learn from these verses?

33. What is the sin of the stronger brother? *1 Corinthians 8:9-12*

34. What is Paul's solution? *1 Corinthians 8:13*

We must be able to rise above our weak brothers' short comings and do what is best for them, putting aside our own personal preferences. Sometimes that means swallowing our pride. Sometimes it means giving in to someone else's idea or spiritual immaturity. And sometimes it means giving up something we might enjoy for the sake of someone else's conscience.

Have you ever heard someone say, if they don't like it, oh well, or too bad for them, or they'll just have to get over it? These are the attitudes Jesus tells us we must change. When we get high and mighty and don't care about others, it is easy to hurt them, or persuade them to go against their conscience and sin (1 Corinthians 8:12). This is where one's humility is tested and measured. When our prideful hearts cause us to do or say hurtful things to a weaker brother, which in turn makes him lose faith in the Savior or sin, then we are the cause of their sin and are better off dead, according to Jesus.

35. Re-write the second half of Matthew 18:6 using your own words in a present day metaphor.

36. According to verse 6 how many people does one have to offend to bring about the wrath of Jesus?

Jesus is passionate as He completes His thoughts on humility. He explains that if anyone's pride and arrogance should ever hurt and cause a humble brother or sister to sin, death by drowning would be far better than the punishment which awaits him.

The disciples had to have been taken aback when Jesus told them they had to change or they would not enter the kingdom of heaven. And again, when He told them they were better off dead and at the bottom of the sea than to live and damage a humble Christian.

We sisters know humility is expected of us today. We know better than to toot our own horn in the church. But we often times don't see that how we treat others is an outward measure of our true humility.

The apostles did finally learn humility, and the church has thrived and grown because of it. And it will continue to thrive and grow when we can truly see others as more important than ourselves.

Listen again to the words of Jesus and think of any changes you might need to make in your attitude to become the humble child God wants you to be.

> *"I tell you the truth, unless you change and become like little children you will never enter the kingdom of heaven. Therefore, whoever humbles himself like this child is the greatest . . ." Matthew 18:3-4*

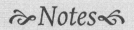

Faith – Part One — Lesson Three

"I tell you the truth, if anyone says to this mountain, 'Go, throw yourself into the sea,' and does not doubt in his heart … it will be done for him." –Mark 11:23

Have you ever witnessed a giant faith firsthand? Have you ever been called on to exemplify a giant faith? We're talking about a faith that has never wavered, never doubted, never given up on God. It is possible for all of us to have a faith like that. And the wonderful news is we do not have to be a super scholar, or be approached by an angel in order to attain it. We only need to believe in and be faithful to the Word of God.

In this lesson, Jesus is speaking about a faith so strong one can command a mountain to get up and throw itself into the sea and not doubt for a moment that it would obey.

Now, who doesn't want a faith like that? But unfortunately, this kind of faith does not just happen when we become a Christian. We must diligently desire it and then purposely cultivate and develop it. This process begins when we actively seek God's will in our lives. We cannot have faith of this magnitude without knowing God on an intimate level. It is from this relationship that we can know God's will, "His good, pleasing and perfect will" (Romans 12:2). If you have any doubt that God is alive, His promises are true, He sees and knows your troubles, needs and fears, or that He hears and answers every prayer you utter—well, for one thing, that mountain will not budge.

We are all born with an innate faith in God. But somewhere along the way as adults we began to rely upon ourselves and we lose that childlike faith. It then becomes a learning process to build up our faith, put aside our fears, and to trust God completely.

In this lesson, we will explore what it takes to build up and to attain a perfect spiritual faith, a faith that will always please our Father and will move the mountains in our lives.

READ: Mark 11:12-16

Our lesson begins on a Tuesday morning, just before the Last Supper. But to fully understand why Jesus did what He did in this passage, we'll look into the background a little bit. Let's go back two days, to Palm Sunday. Jerusalem would have been filled with sojourners from all over the world making their pilgrimage to celebrate the Passover feast. The temple courtyard was a beehive of activity with everyone busily purchasing their supplies for the celebration. Mark tells us that after the triumphal entry, Jesus made his way to the temple. What He saw taking place there broke His heart, yet He did nothing about it . . . that day.

On Monday morning, while Jesus and His followers were walking back to Jerusalem, Jesus saw a

When Jesus Speaks, Will You Listen?

fig tree and stopped to eat. When He discovered the tree had no figs, He cursed it. Walking on, they again made their way through the crowded streets of Jerusalem into the temple courtyard. Once again Jesus observed the activities going on, and this time, He took action. He began driving out customers, merchants, the sacrificial animals and birds. He knocked over the tables of the foreign exchange agents and the benches of the dove and pigeon sellers. After He drove out all the merchants, He barred the entrances and did not allow merchants back in the courtyard of the temple to conduct business for the rest of the day (Matthew 21:12ff; Mark 11:17ff).

That evening, Jesus and His followers returned to Bethany and spent the night (Matthew 21:17). Early Tuesday morning, they all headed back to Jerusalem. This is where our study will pick up.

READ: Mark 11:20

> 1. Why did the fig tree not have fruit on it? *Mark 11:13*
>
> 2. Write the words Jesus used to curse the fig tree? *Mark 11:14*
>
> 3. What was the condition of the fig tree the next day, after the cursing? *Mark 11:20*

READ: Mark 11:21

> 4. Describe the tone you hear in Peter's voice as he discovers the fig tree. What did Peter find unusual about it?

READ: Mark 11:22

> 5. What is Jesus' answer to Peter's observation of the tree?
>
> 6. What do you make of Jesus' answer to Peter's statement?

At first glance, the clearing of the temple and the cursing of the fig tree may seem disconnected; maybe even a bit of an overreaction on the part of Jesus, like something someone in a really bad mood might do. But Jesus had a very specific purpose in mind for what He did. Jesus used severe measures to make a point. He knew full well that His followers wouldn't understand what He did at first. You have to admit, these two events got everyone's attention, which was precisely what He wanted.

Turning our attention back to the temple, let's look at how it was designed to be used, noticing specifically how it was misused by the Jews.

READ: Mark 11:17

7. What was the purpose of the temple, and who was allowed to use it?

8. What did Jesus say the leaders had made the temple into? What had they done wrong?

READ: Jeremiah 7:9-11

9. What did God say about the temple?

10. Setting the buying and selling aside, what were the people doing wrong at the temple in Jeremiah's day? With what attitude was God displeased?

The temple was supposed to be used as a house of prayer for ALL nations (Mark 11:17). The temple courtyard was designated for that specific purpose. But the Jewish leaders were using it, and allowing others to use it, for monetary gain. During this holiday time, buying Passover items and exchanging foreign money for visitors was commonplace at the temple, so much so that no one thought anything wrong with using this portion of the temple as a marketplace. They were conducting business as usual as they carelessly disobeyed God. Just as thieves lose sight of the evil of their ill-gotten gains, and jubilantly enjoy their treasures, so were the Jewish merchants and customers.

> **11. Name the various activities going on at the temple during Passover week. You may want to use a Bible dictionary or commentary.** *Mark 11:15-17*

Passover was just days away and many foreigners came to Jerusalem for their yearly sacrifice. The temple was bursting with Jewish merchants looking forward to making money from these pilgrims. Money exchangers were there to exchange the visitor's foreign currency into a temple currency that the visitor could use to pay the temple tax and to purchase an animal for sacrifice. Merchants eagerly accommodated customers needing flawless animals, doves or pigeons for sacrifice. Others sought a clay pot in which to roast their Passover lamb. Whatever their need, it could be found and purchased in the temple courtyard, often at exorbitant prices.

All this commotion was taking place in the courtyard of the Gentiles, the largest area in the temple, the very place marked for non-Jews to come worship God.

READ: Mark 11:18

> **12. What was the reaction of the religious leaders after Jesus cleared the temple?**
>
> **13. What do you believe amazed the crowd?**

Jesus knew that turning over the money changers' tables and driving out the animals and merchants would offend and infuriate many Jews. He realized fully the impact His actions would have on both those who followed Him, and those who opposed Him.

The witnesses in Jesus' day didn't understand why He cleared the temple or why He cursed the fig tree. Those who were not angry, were bewildered and confused to say the least. But Jesus was in full control. He knew their reactions would be extreme. In acting in these unexpected ways, Jesus was able to grab everyone's attention and teach a lesson they were not expecting, but would be vital for generations to come. These events were symbolic acts of a judgment that God would bestow soon, and Jesus needed the Jews to pay attention and to think.

14. What does Jesus warn would become of the temple in Mark 13:2?

15. In your opinion, why were the Jewish leaders more at fault for the misuse of the temple than the merchants or customers?

Though Jesus was not understood in *His* day, His point is clear to us today. God's judgment on the corrupt spiritual leaders of Jesus' day would be carried out through the destruction of their own icon, the temple. It is important to remember that there was nothing wrong with the temple itself. It would be judged and destroyed because of the way in which the spiritual leaders were misusing it, swearing by it, and allowing others to misplace their faith in God with faith in the temple itself.

16. Who was commanded to pay the temple tax? How much was it? *Exodus 30:11-16.*

17. What did Jesus say about paying the temple tax? *Matthew 17:24-26*

18. What was the objection of Jesus toward those buying and selling at the temple? *Mark 11:15-17*

Jesus did not have a problem with people paying the temple tax, nor did He have a problem with them purchasing animals to sacrifice. But He did have a problem with the way the religious leaders were using the court of the Gentiles. He did not approve of them taking over the area of the temple that was meant for worship and turning it into a marketplace. And without a hint of shame, they ignored the word of God and used the temple grounds as they pleased.

Both the clearing of the temple and cursing the fig tree were symbolic of God's judgment on Israel's spiritual leaders for their gross misuse of the temple and for not producing the intended fruit. The temple and the fig tree were both found barren, and therefore worthless to those for whom they existed. Jesus' followers would have to put their faith in something other than the temple. A new day was dawning! They would have to replace the faith they had in the temple with faith in God alone. There would be no need of the temple hierarchical priesthood with it's list of man-made traditions when the new church was established.

> **19 Write a brief definition of the word FAITH. You may want to use a Bible dictionary.**
>
> **20. For what were our first century brothers commended?** *Hebrews 11:1-2*
>
> **21. Explain what Paul means in 2 Corinthians 5:7.**

Now the words Jesus spoke to Peter in regard to the withered fig tree in Mark 11:22, "Have faith in God." make perfect sense. It was men ignoring the Lord's instructions that caused the temple to be destroyed. The temple had been around for hundreds of years in Jesus' day and was an integral part of every Jewish person's life. It was a place of safety and for many a false sense of righteousness just by being at it. Even today, you'll find many worshipers at the Western Wall or the Wailing Wall praying to God, hopelessly believing God will be more attentive to their prayers because of their proximity to the ancient ruins.

Destroying the temple will shake the faith of many, and in so doing, cause them to question their spiritual leaders who had taught them to use it for solace, to swear by it, and misuse it. And ultimately, it will cause them to put their faith in God and the unseen.

> **22. After Solomon had dedicated the temple, what did God tell him would become of it if he or his sons did not follow His commands?** *1 Kings 9:6-8*
>
> **23. Why did God say He would reject the temple?** *1 Kings 9:9*

 *READ: Mark 11:23a*

24. In Mark 11:23 and Matthew 19:26, who or what is the power behind moving a mountain? Explain your answer.

Jesus used the phrase, "mountains being thrown into the sea" purposely. It was a common saying or idiom in biblical times and would be easily understood by everyone.

25. What do these passages have to say about mountains being moved and man's faith in God?

Psalm 46:2b

1 Corinthians 13:2

In His use of this idiom, Jesus is referring to a common figure of speech that His listeners knew and understood well. By the connotation of the old phrase used by the Psalmist and again by Paul, we know Jesus was not speaking of mountains being tossed about, but rather He was speaking of the power of God being demonstrated through a person of faith. But let's read on and we'll see there is a catch; something one must have in order to move mountains.

 *READ: Mark 11:23b*

26. What is Jesus implying man has doubts about?

When we ask of God, we must not doubt His capability or depth of concern. Moving a mountain is God's power demonstrated through a faithful follower. It is not the power of a faithful follower's prayer. (Albeit, God does work His power through our prayers, but that's another lesson.) Faith does not doubt that God can do what we ask. It doesn't limit God, nor question His ability to carry out His promises. Faith completely acknowledges the fact that God is omnipotent, all powerful, just as we did when we were children.

Let's explore for a moment the reason one doubts in the first place. It seems so simple a promise that God will take care of us and will not give us more than we can bear (1 Corinthians 10:13). Yet, instead of clinging to these reassuring promises, we choose to worry and fret in place of clinging to God's Word. Why do we do this?

Sarah reasoned with her limited human understanding and it drew her to the conclusion that she must have a child her own way rather than wait on God and trust in His promise to her. Look at Eve walking along with God daily, yet was so easily manipulated into reasoning that a piece of fruit looking and smelling so good could not be bad for her. Both of these women knew what God had said, and both decided they knew better. They balanced their own logic and rationale against God's, and presumed they were right. Why not use our own intellect and reasoning to figure out our problem, you might ask. That's a fair question.

27. What does the Proverb writer admonish us to do? What does he warn us not to do? Explain. *Proverbs 3:5-7*

28. In what ways do we conform to the world? *Romans 12:2*

29. What does it mean to renew our minds and how does one do it? *Romans 12:2*

30. According to Paul, what are two ways we have of thinking through a problem or difficulty? *1 Corinthians 2:13-15*

31. Why does man find it so hard to accept the Word of God? *1 Corinthians 2:14.*

Man's wisdom can be very convincing at times. It is easy to understand why many fell for it in the Bible. We have looked at Eve and Sarah, but Abraham too used man's logic. He got himself in trouble with Pharaoh and Abimelech when he did not trust God, but came up with his own plan to

Lesson 3: Faith, Part One

save his life (Genesis 12:11-13 & 20:2-11). We see Jonah hearing God's instructions and carrying out what his human reason told him would be a better idea. We must never ever think we are smarter than God or that God doesn't know what He is talking about this one time. Peter was rebuked by Jesus for thinking he knew best.

> **32. What did Jesus think of Peter's human logic? Explain.** *Mark 8:33*

As we contemplate our own situations, trials, tests, and struggles, we must keep the words of God in our minds and act on them. Oftentimes, the world tells us one thing while God is telling us another. Look at the conclusion of the world when it comes to evolution, abortion, homosexuality, morals, raising children, revenge—the list is unending. The point is, we must train our minds to think differently than the world on a myriad of situations. The world is dead wrong on so many things and we must not fall into its trap of illogical, ungodly or politically correct reasoning and rationale. Jesus is calling us to ignore the world, have faith in God alone, and move those mountains with God's wisdom and power. I'd like to see the world do that!

Our renewed mind will help us decipher the world's reasoning, logic and wisdom and lead us to know that God will take care of us (1 Peter 5:7); that He won't give us more than we can bear; *I Corinthians 10:13* and that Jesus gives us strength to do everything we are called to do (Philippians 4:13). So if I begin to worry, stress or fret, I am literally rejecting God's promises, joining my sisters Eve and Sarah, and seeking my own desire over God's. I'm agreeing with the world that God can not handle my problems.

> **33. What is Paul's dilemma in Romans 7:21-25? Where was the war fought?**

READ: Romans 8:5-8

> **34. What are the two things one can have his mind set on?**

> **35. Explain where the hostility comes from.**

> **36. Which choice pleases God? Why is that so?**

When Jesus Speaks, Will You Listen?

Paul points out such a relevant truth for us today. Our minds still work in the same manner as our brothers' and sisters' in Jesus' day. We fight the same war in our minds as they did. Our desires and passions are telling us one way to think, while God is telling us something entirely different.

> **37. According to Paul, how is the battle in our minds to be fought? How does one do that?**
> *2 Corinthians 10:5*

**READ: Mark 11:23**

Jesus is calling us to have a perfect faith; a faith which is confident and doubtless that trusts and believes every promise of God verbatim. This kind of faith doesn't happen overnight. It is somewhat of a two steps forward one step back type journey. Even though we work mightily at it, we still fall short at times. But take heart, even the apostles and followers of Jesus had their weak moments of doubt.

Let's look at a few instances in the lives of the disciples and see where their faith was destroyed by doubt, a time when their faith did not move mountains. We will see how Jesus responds to such doubt and faithlessness. Notice the strong reproof of Jesus as He rebukes His followers. Also notice the thought process as the world's rationale influenced the disciples' reactions which led to their distrust in God.

> **38. In each of these passages look for: 1) who doubted Jesus; 2) why they doubted Him; and 3) how Jesus responded to them.**
>
> *Matthew 14:29-31*
>
> *Mark 4:35-41*
>
> *Luke 12:28-30*

One may look at these events and wonder how the apostles and followers of Jesus could ever doubt Him. But haven't we done the same thing? We can have all the faith in the world until something bad happens. Instead of trusting and relying on God and His promises, we fearfully panic and worry. Our faith, when at the point of doubt, seems to be more a mere knowledge of God with zero trust in Him. When this is the case, it raises the question, is one's faith real. Do we believe and trust God or not.

39. Look at these promises of God. Explain what trials each passage will help one through.

Luke 18:27

1 Corinthians 10:13

Philippians 4:13

Hebrews 13:5

40. What promise of God do you hold most dear? Perhaps you hold on to one not mentioned above.

Having faith in God, the kind that pleases Him, is a faith that will hold on to God's promises to take care of you, give you the strength you will need for every task, and bring you through unbearable circumstances. God either will do that, or He has lied. And we know God cannot lie (Hebrews 6:18). So we must conclude God will carry and help us through each and every trial, problem, test and circumstance. To believe anything short of that is doubting. He will help us raise our children, find a job, retire on little, live without our loved one and make ends meet! It may not be instant or easy, He may have to say wait, but He promises to be there for us through thick and thin. It has been said, "God is rarely early, but always on time."

We must constantly keep our own logical thinking and rationale in control as we compare it to the promises of God. Remember Eve was only deceived when she decided the fruit looked and smelled too good to be bad for her. Her desirous rationale changed her life forever.

We are going to stop here and think on these things for a while. Next, we will look at some faith heroes of the Bible. Some were faith giants while others fell short. We'll look at some practical things we can do to help us grow closer to God and build an even stronger faith that does not doubt and can move mountains.

Faith Part Two — Lesson Four

"I tell you the truth, if anyone says to this mountain, 'go, throw yourself into the sea,' and does not doubt in his heart ... it will be done for him." –Mark 11:23

In your mind what makes a person's faith great? I'm talking about a faith that is unfazed in situations where the strongest of the faithful would cave. Someone with a faith so strong they might even laugh at the thought of death, because of the joy they know awaits them on the other side. Or their trust in the sheer fact that God is in control makes them fearless.

Today, we're going to look at occurrences in the Bible when followers of Jesus stood the test, and other times when they failed their test of faith. You and I are like the church folks in the first century in every way. They succumbed to the same pressures as you and I. In their moments of weakness they responded to the voice of human rationale or personal desire instead of standing on the promises of God.

In this lesson, we will be looking at three biblical accounts of faith. In each example, we will learn some do's and don'ts that will help us grow our faith into a giant faith.

1) PETER' WALKS ON WATER

READ: Matthew 14:29-31

> **1. What sort of tasks or ministries do you fear?**

Have you ever found yourself saying, "Yes, I will do that," only to wonder what in the world you got yourself into when the time came to carry out the obligation? We start a task with great confidence only to be weighted down with the fear of failure. We lose confidence, which happens when our confidence is in ourself, and not in God.

Peter was brave—the bravest man in the boat. No one else volunteered to step out into the raging water. Our hero was a shining example of faith; he was stepping out of his comfort zone, doing something he had never done before, until he looked at the storm. His reaction when he saw the water reveals the source of Peter's confidence. But notice Jesus did not reprimand Peter for failing to stay on top of the water. But rather, He was upset with Peter for not trusting Him after he had made the choice to try.

When we become fearful and lose faith, it isn't ourselves we are losing faith in at all. Do you see that? Peter wasn't chastised for loosing faith in himself, but rather for losing faith in Jesus. Jesus didn't say, "Peter, you should have more confidence yourself!" When we begin to fear our own failure, we are actually doubting God's power to work through us.

Faith that doubts God, cannot move a mountain. Real faith does not fear failure when faced with a task or situation which stretches one's talents, abilities or experience, but rather it embraces the promise of God to always be there giving the strength needed (Philippians 4:13).

Fear of failing at a task that you are capable of accomplishing is a reflection of your faith in God, not yourself. Now, this does of course have its limits. We must have a little talent in an area before taking on a challenge. Someone without medical training would not enter an operating room and perform brain surgery. However, a school teacher could take on the challenge of teaching a Bible class. Peter, full of trust in Jesus, took on a task, lost confidence in himself, failed the task and disappointed His Lord.

2. Explain the difference in doubting God, and doubting one's own abilities.

3. How does Philippians 4:13 encourage you to use your talents and abilities?

4. Explain how a fear of failure is a lack of faith in God.

2) THE APOSTLES FEAR OF THE STORM
The second biblical account is a test of faith many Christians struggle with: fear of death and of difficult and unforeseen circumstances.

**READ:** Mark 4:35-41

5. List the kinds of things most Christians tend to fear.

6. Is there a fear or anxiety that is not covered by Philippians 4:6-7? What does Paul tell us to do with our fears and anxieties?

7. How does fearing unchangeable circumstances demonstrate a lack of faith? Is fear and worry always a lack of faith?

8. What question do the disciples frantically ask Jesus in Mark 4:38? Underline the words you think the disciples might have emphasized.

9. Write out the question Jesus asked his disciples in Mark 4:40. Underline the words you think Jesus emphasized.

Have you ever in your heart of hearts heard Jesus say those words to you? Why are you so afraid, really why? Do you still have no faith, none at all?

Our personal fears are a real test and also a measure of our faith. Oftentimes our worst fears do come true: our loved ones do not get better, we do not get the job we hoped for, our family member or friend does let us down. What then do we conclude: God isn't there when we need Him or that He lets us down, or like the apostles, He doesn't care what happens to us? No, the answer is always: God will NEVER let you down. He does what an omniscient God does. He does what is best according to His wisdom. Can we accept that, even in dire circumstances? Do we believe that no matter the outcome, God is in complete control?

When Jesus Speaks, Will You Listen?

The apostles were afraid for their lives during the terrifying storm and had given up hope in God taking care of them as they grabbed the buckets and bailed water. We can know this by the way they spoke to Jesus in their utter despair, "Don't you care if we drown?" In response, Jesus seems just as upset with them when He asks, "Do you *still* have no faith? (Mark 4:38, 40)"

Have you ever felt like you were drowning and that God just didn't care? In these moments, we need to pause and allow the words that Jesus spoke to Peter resonate in our hearts, "Have faith in God." Real faith looks to God for help, wisdom, or courage; and then, most importantly, trusts God to carry out His will by accepting what happens to be His answer. We are talking about giant faith here!

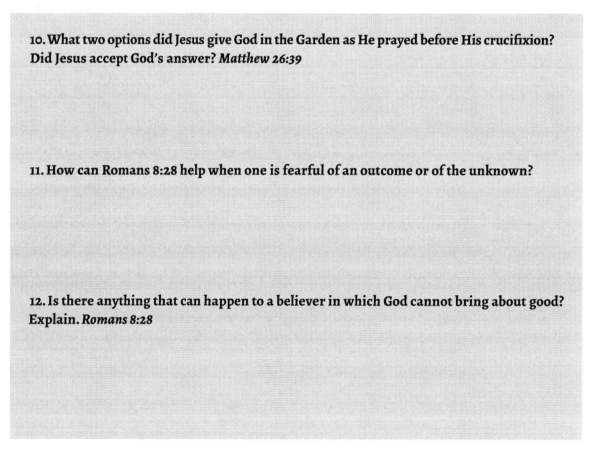

10. What two options did Jesus give God in the Garden as He prayed before His crucifixion? Did Jesus accept God's answer? *Matthew 26:39*

11. How can Romans 8:28 help when one is fearful of an outcome or of the unknown?

12. Is there anything that can happen to a believer in which God cannot bring about good? Explain. *Romans 8:28*

Next time you are fearful of an outcome, have faith in God. Express yourself in prayer, and then let your Sovereign Lord take over from there. Is that always easy to do? No. Do we enjoy seeing opportunities pass us by, being hurt and disappointed by those we love or watching a loved one die? By no means! But allowing God the option to carry out His will (which may be the opposite of our will) is the only option for a faithful child of God. And the truth is, knowing our Father is aware and concerned about our situation and that He will handle it for us, gets us through the ordeal with tranquil peace and comfort (Philippians 4:7). Perfect faith trusts God to handle our problems according to His perfect will. It also means deferring our own desire and will to His.

The third event we'll look at really hits home and seems impossible to do at times, but with a little faith and a lot of prayer, we can master it.

3) SERMON ON THE MOUNT—WORRY

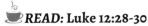READ: Luke 12:28-30

13. What were the followers of Jesus worrying about? What specifically do you worry about?

Is there anyone who has not worried? We seem unable to help ourselves. Yet, when we hear the reaction of Jesus toward those who worry, we can't help but feel ashamed of our lack of faith.

14. How is worrying a sign of a lack of faith in God?

15. Explain the logic of Jesus on the subject of worry in Luke 12:25-26.

16. What reassurance does Jesus give to enforce the fact that one should not worry? *Matthew 6:32*

17. Explain the concluding words of Jesus on worry in Matthew 6:34.

When Jesus Speaks, Will You Listen?

Now, okay, let's all admit it, to worry is always a distrust in the power of our Heavenly Father. It doesn't matter what we are worried about. To doubt God will take care of the things we pray for indicates a lack of faith. If we cannot trust God to handle our problems for us, or if we think He is just not hearing us, really and truly we are displaying NO faith at all. God promises to take care of us; Jesus said God already knows what we need before we even ask Him (Matthew 6:8). He either does know, or Jesus is lying. We may want to throw in a shade of gray here, thinking our problem is unique, but there really is no gray. This is as black and white as it sounds.

Perfect faith does not worry about the future, but trusts God to do what is right even if the answer is no, especially when we do not know where our next meal will come from, what will become of our loved one, how we will pay our bills, or how we will ever retire. Faith is not faith if we can see the answer. God expects us to trust Him without understanding or agreeing with His reasoning. Jesus told Peter at the fig tree and is telling us today to "have faith in God" even when we cannot see the rhyme or reason or like the final outcome, *and* to do so without doubting! That means having complete confidence in God's judgment at all times.

18. What does 1 Peter 5:7 tell us to do with our worries and anxiety?

19. In Philippians 4:6-7 what are we told God will do if we present our problems to Him? What does that mean?

Most Christians believe God is in control of the world, but some doubt He is in control of *their* life. They are a like child who brags about his dad's strength and his huge muscles but is too afraid to jump from a tree branch into his arms. Admitting God is all powerful, but being unwilling to hand over our problems is—well, "O you of little faith," there will be no mountains moving for you.

READ: Mark 11:20-23 again

Jesus told Peter to "have faith in God." He means enough faith to believe without any physical evidence that God will take care of whatever we ask of Him. What God did to that fig tree, and what He was going to do to the temple, was effortless for Him. Our God can do anything! Even take care of our problems in life.

The Bible is full of brave men and women who trusted God without doubting. Let's look at a few examples of real and powerful faith, faith in which God was well pleased.

20. How did these characters exemplify their faith?

   ABEL: *Hebrews 11:4 & Genesis 4:4*

   NOAH: *Hebrews 11:7 & Genesis 6:13-22*

   ABRAHAM: *Hebrews 11:8, 11, 17 & Genesis 22:1-11*

   MOSES: *Hebrews 11:23-24*

   JOSEPH: *Genesis 45:3; 50:20*

   SHADRACH, MESHACH, and ABEDNEGO: *Daniel 3:18*

These great men of faith are our heroes because they did what most of us will not do. They trusted God without any explanation or knowledge of how things would turn out. They did not fear their future, their own failure or even death. This is the faith Jesus is talking about, the kind that can move mountains. Their faith caused them to trust in God as they: crossed seas on dry land, walked through fire, survived a flood, and carried on when displaced.

The writer of Hebrews, in chapter 11, gives a glowing report of men and women who lived faithful lives, trusting God through all their perils. You don't see Abraham paralyzed from indecision over whether or not to follow God's will and sacrifice his son, Joseph battling bitterness because he grew up away from his family, Moses going into a tizzy because he didn't know what would happen at the Red Sea, or Shadrach and his friends buckling under pressure to conform. No,

When Jesus Speaks, Will You Listen?

these heroes trusted God with their very lives. They didn't just talk about their faith, they lived it out. And as a result, men wrote about them, we admire them, and God was pleased with them.

21. What does the Proverb writer tell us about faith in God in Proverbs 3:5? Explain.

22. Why is it impossible to please God without faith? (Don't you just wish at times that wasn't true?) *Hebrews 11:6*

23. Read Hebrews 10:36-38. What does it mean to live by faith? What happens to those who don't live by faith?

Our heroes of old are perfect examples of what real faith looks like. They lived their lives with one purpose in mind; to please God, not themselves, just God. They didn't doubt or fret over whether God heard their prayers. They didn't worry and second-guess God when He gave them His answer, even though it was not the answer they were looking for. They didn't try and change God's command, nor did they ever doubt His existence or His omnipotent power.

Now, let's not confuse belief in God's existence with having faith in Him. They are two entirely different things. It is possible to know God lives, but not have faith in Him. Sadly, there are a lot of believers today who do not know the difference. What set our heroes and heroines apart from their contemporaries and got their names in the Hebrews book of "Who's Who," was their ability to live a faithful life as they followed God's will, and never doubted Him, even during their many struggles, trials and sufferings.

24. What do we have in common with the demons? *James 2:19*

25. What do demons fear? *James 2:19*

26. Explain how it is possible to know God exists, but not have faith in Him.

27. What are the two prerequisites to having faith according to Hebrews 11:6?

Like our faithful brothers and sisters of old, God still longs for you and me to demonstrate our faith by being strong when trials come and by not doubting Him or the fact that He is in control of our situations. This faithfulness pleases Him, and I'm sure it makes Him smile.

True faith cannot be measured by our attendance. Even the faithless attend services. It can't be measured by the things we do. We can do all kinds of good things with improper motives. Nor is one's knowledge of God a measurement of faith. Even demons know things about our Father.

28. Explain what is being said of the Law and faith in Galatians 3:11.

29. What does Peter say is the goal of our faith? *1 Peter 1:6-7*

With just a little bit of faith, "If you have faith as small as a mustard seed," Jesus said in Luke 17:6, you can accomplish so much. This lesson is not an easy 1-2-3, but calls each of us to honestly search our hearts and see if we are lacking in our faith, or if it is growing day by day as we faithfully depend on the Lord. It can be a struggle at times to trust and not doubt, especially when we want our way badly, but it is such a blessing, comfort and peace when we do.

> **30. What do these passages teach about faith and its reward?**
>
> *2 Timothy 4:7-8*
>
> *James 1:12*
>
> *Revelation 2:10*

A crown of life is what every faithful believer longs for. We all want a faith that will keep us strong when we can't see the light at the end of the tunnel, give us peace during impossible trials, make us strong when we are weak, and give us courage when we otherwise would be scared out of our mind. We want to trust God to carry out His will even though we do not see His entire plan and strategy. Have you ever told your children, "Just trust me"? We expect them to believe us and just take our word for things they can't understand, and they do. That is what Jesus was trying to get through to His followers that day at the fig tree. Never mind how things look, or what you want, or how scared you are—just trust in God. That's it, just trust in God at all times.

And now as we look back to that day in Jerusalem and consider the smallness of a mustard seed, and as we contemplate our own faith, I want you to imagine Jesus speaking these words to you, "Have faith in God, and you too can move mountains."

"I tell you the truth, if anyone says to this mountain, 'go, throw yourself into the sea,' and does not doubt in his heart . . . it will be done for him." Mark 11:23

Holy Spirit — Lesson Five

"But I tell you the truth: it is for your good that I am going away. Unless I go away, the Counselor will not come to you; but if I go, I will send Him to you." –John 16:7

The Holy Spirit, what a vast and often mysterious subject. In our study this week we will look at some characteristics of the Spirit. We will consider who He is, what His purpose on earth has been and how He works in our lives today.

The role of the Holy Spirit changed after Jesus ascended into heaven. He had always been active, but after the day of Pentecost in Acts 2, He literally entered into the hearts of believers, giving them strength, wisdom, peace, and guidance.

The apostles had their doubts when Jesus explained they would be better off once He was gone and the Counselor came. Two thousand years later we can read the account in John 16 and understand that Jesus did have to leave this earth in order for the Spirit to come. And we know that the Spirit did indeed come after Jesus ascended into heaven.

Though a person may know intellectually that the Spirit is real, it is not the same as fully understanding His purpose. We may know He is here with us, but not understand exactly what He does for every believer. Jesus is about to change all of that.

In the opening scene of today's lesson we find Jesus in a conversation with the apostles. They had just finished their Passover meal and were getting ready to leave the upper room and go to that quiet place they all knew and loved in the Garden of Gethsemane. Let's listen in as Jesus explains the new work of the Holy Spirit, the Counselor who was to come to the apostles and to all believers.

Read: John 16:7-14

But, before we begin our lesson, a little background information will remind us of how the Holy Spirit accomplished His work before Jesus ascended into heaven.

> **1. The first mention of the Holy Spirit is in Genesis 1:2. What do we find Him doing?**

When Jesus Speaks, Will You Listen?

The Holy Spirit, the Spirit of God and the Spirit are mentioned over 200 times in the Old Testament. The next few questions will deal with the various ways in which the Spirit worked in the lives of God's people from creation to the time of Jesus.

> **2. According to these passages, how did the Spirit work, and in whom did the Spirit work?**
>
> *Exodus 31:1-3*
>
> *1 Samuel 19:23*
>
> *2 Samuel 23:2*
>
> *Nehemiah 9:30*
>
> *Isaiah 63:11-12, 14*
>
> *Ezekiel 36:27*
>
> *Daniel 5:11-14*

There are numerous accounts of the Holy Spirit's involvement in the Old Testament. The exercise above demonstrates a variety of ways in which the Spirit used man to bring about God's will. The Holy Spirit was used to deliver God's wayward Israelites, control a crisis and empower men and women with various abilities. In those days God used priests, judges, kings, prophets, old, young, male and female to accomplish His purpose. The Spirit would come for a limited time and work through individuals chosen by God, instructing and enabling them to carry out the Lord's plan, and then be gone for a time.

In the New Testament, the Spirit continued to work through specific individuals. He was active in the life of Elizabeth and Zechariah at the birth of their son, John the Baptist. He overshadowed

Mary, and she became pregnant with the Son of God. The Spirit was actively involved in the life of Jesus, as well as His forerunner and cousin, John the Baptist. The Spirit was there fulfilling prophecy during the baptism of Jesus and throughout His ministry. But it was not until Jesus left the earth and ascended into heaven that the Holy Spirit's role changed and He began to do all that He does today (Luke 1:67-79 & Matthew 3:16).

The apostles did not like the idea of Jesus leaving them. Jesus tried to explain to them that things really would be better for them after He was gone. But they just couldn't believe it, or understand it completely, until He was gone and the Comforter had come.

With this in mind, let's jump into our story and see what Jesus had to say about this wonderful Counselor whom we all desire to live within us.

READ: John 16:7

3. Why did Jesus say He must go away?

4. According to John 7:38-39, when would the Spirit come?

5. How long will the Counselor be with us, and what is He called in John 14:16-17?

6. What does Jesus say the Counselor will do in John 15:26?

As we listen to Jesus telling His apostles they would be better off once He was glorified and with the Father, we can sense their bewilderment. They were so distraught by the fact that Jesus would leave them that they didn't even ask Him where He was going (John 16:5). The Apostles couldn't fathom how their lives could be better with Jesus gone. Much like we cannot imagine how heaven can be better than our life on earth (though we trust it will be!).

The Holy Spirit had to wait until Jesus was gone and at the right hand of God before He could make His appearance (Luke 22:69). And what a glorious, grand appearance He made!

When Jesus Speaks, Will You Listen?

7. How did the apostles receive the Spirit? How did everyone else receive Him?
Acts 2:1-4; 2:38-39

The Christian world was forever changed on that momentous day—the day of Pentecost. From that moment on there was a distinct division between the Jews who believed Jesus was the Messiah and the Jews who did not. A brand-new life had begun for those first believers who put their faith in the risen Son of God. And a brand-new church had begun that was made up of Christians who shared a common belief that Jesus was their long awaited Messiah. No longer would they need to sacrifice animals for sins, nor would they need a priest to intercede on their behalf. The new Christians now had a Counselor, a Comforter, and an Advisor who lived right inside of them! The religion they had practiced for thousands and thousands of years was changed forever on this historic day (Galatians 3:5, 11, 13).

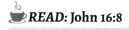READ: John 16:8

8. What did Jesus say the Spirit would do?

9. In what three areas will the Spirit convict the world?

1.

2.

3.

10. Name some practical ways the Spirit works in our lives to convict us of sin.

52   *Lesson 5: Holy Spirit*

The Spirit knows each of us and works uniquely in every individual to do whatever it takes to convict that person of sin and convince them of who Jesus is. Once a person is convicted of their sin and repents, they still have another step to take in order to receive the Holy Spirit, this Counselor whom Jesus promised. Let's go back to Jerusalem to the day of Pentecost and see what the Apostle Peter told the crowd to do.

While Peter was preaching in Acts 2, the Spirit who had filled the apostles in the upper room just hours before was working in the hearts and minds of those in the crowd. As Peter preached, some in the audience began to feel the prodding of the Holy Spirit on their conscience. At the end of Peter's sermon we can see how the Spirit had affected the audience by their reaction.

11. How did the crowd react to Peter's message? *Acts 2:37*

12. What did Peter tell the people they must do to be saved in Acts 2:38?

13. What two promises did the followers receive upon baptism? *Acts 2:38*

After Jesus ascended into heaven He did indeed send the Holy Spirit to work in the hearts and minds of believers. He launched into motion the active indwelling work of the Holy Spirit in the lives of those who believed. By God's divine design, the Spirit works in us today, convincing us of our need for forgiveness and for Christ in our lives. Once He convicts us of our sin and need of a Savior, Peter tells us it is through our obedience in baptism that we receive the Holy Spirit. Our conversion process and the transformation that takes place in our lives is known as regeneration. Paul speaks of the regenerating work of the Holy Spirit in Romans 6:3ff, Colossians 2:12 and Titus 3:5-6.

14. What does Paul teach us concerning the Holy Spirit in these passages?

   Romans 8:9

   1 Corinthians 6:19

   2 Timothy 1:14

When Jesus Speaks, Will You Listen?

What an awesome design of God to send His Holy Spirit to convict unbelievers. Without the Spirit in our lives, we would never be free from the hold Satan has on us. Once the Spirit convicts us of our sin and we repent, we must be baptized. It is through baptism that we acquire the indwelling of the Spirit (*Acts 2:38*).

At the same time the Spirit is carrying out His work of convicting the world of their guilt and sin, Satan is actively trying to stop Him. The Spirit's work can be very difficult because our human nature longs to indulge in its selfish desires. No one has to twist our arm to make us self-centered and self-indulgent. We love pampering ourselves with every pleasure we can afford. Satan's words tickle our ears with suggestive ideas that turn us away from God. Thankfully, the Spirit is diligent in His loving ministry. We have all witnessed the Spirit at work in our own lives and in the lives of our unbelieving friends and family as He directs His loved ones away from sin.

Sadly, there are times when unbelievers and believers alike choose to ignore and turn away from the Spirit's conviction and encouragement. They'd rather tune in to the "easy listening" of Satan.

15. What do these passages say we are able to do in regard to ignoring the Holy Spirit?

Acts 7:51

Ephesians 4:30

1 Thessalonians 5:19

16. Explain what it means to resist, grieve and put out the fire of the Holy Spirit. Then give an example of how one can do that today.

Resist:

Example:

Grieve:

Example:

Quench:

Example:

God has mercifully given the world the Holy Spirit. Without Him we would never admit our faults, see our sins or feel our guilt. Yet, the work of the Spirit is limited, He does not force anyone to listen or comply or obey Him. We each choose whether to listen and conform to the Spirit, or to continue in our sin. Both believers and unbelievers have the option and the power to harden their hearts with self-deceit and ignorant rationalization.

READ: John 16:9

17. Finish the sentence of Jesus: "In regard to sin, _____".

18. What is the difference in not knowing who Jesus is and not believing in Jesus? Why is it a sin?

19. What will happen to those who do not believe in Jesus? *John 8:24*

The Holy Spirit works hard to help us know Jesus. Yet, one's desire to be self-sufficient and not listen is a worldwide trait. Our human nature hungrily listens to Satan as he tells us why we don't need God. And that, dear sisters, is why we need the Holy Spirit convincing us otherwise.

The Counselor helps unbelievers see the fallacy in thinking that they can love Jesus while continuing to sin. But being convicted of our sin is just one aspect of guilt the Counselor brings to our attention. Let's go on to the second.

READ: John 16:10

20. What is the second aspect of conviction Jesus speaks of? Why is it important?

When Jesus Speaks, Will You Listen?

Jesus knew the apostles would need spiritual help to keep themselves righteous once He was gone. It was hard enough for the apostles to remain righteous and holy with Jesus present, so when He was gone—well, they were going to need some help, as we all do.

> **21. Write a definition for the word righteousness using your own words.**
>
>
>
> **22. How does the Spirit help us remain righteous?**
>
> *Romans 8:26*
>
>
> *Romans 8:26-27*
>
>
> *1 Corinthians 2:12*
>
>
> *Ephesians 3:16*

God's people have always needed His guidance to live a righteous life. We just do not have it in our human DNA to transform our minds and live holy lives without the aid of the Spirit. But now we have Him living in us, giving us strength and power to overcome all sin and temptation in our lives. If that is not enough, He comes to our aid in our weakest moments and talks to our Father on our behalf in a dialect known only to them.

The Comforter is always working in us to either convict us of our sin, convince us of our need to know who Jesus is, or help us become the holy and righteous daughters we were created to be. One of the ways He accomplishes the latter is to work in each individual Christian, helping to develop the character traits needed to overcome a trial. Using these traits He directs believers to others who are seeking God, or need comfort, help or encouragement, as well as friends facing difficult situations in their lives. He is the one bringing folks who have a need, to those who have a solution. He busily orchestrates these encounters.

> **23. Name the fruit (character traits) the Spirit helps us develop.** *Galatians 5:22-23*
>
> 1.

2.

3.

4.

5.

6.

7.

8.

9.

24. In what way does the Spirit help us develop these traits?

25. Go back to Question 23 and put a check next to the fruit you have personally felt the nudge of the Spirit working within you to develop either currently or in the past. If you can think of a specific incident, add a short title on the line.

Without the aid of the Holy Spirit we would all be doomed sinners. We would not and could not pull ourselves away from sin; we would not even try. The Spirit does not only point out our sins, but He helps us remain faithful, righteous and holy in our everyday lives. He gives us the desire and the will to be what God wants us to be. And because of His work in us, we are confident in our walk with God, assured that we can be loving, joyful, peacemaking, patient, kind, good, faithful, gentle and self-controlled daughters of God! Wow, what a blessing, what a comfort!

26. How does John describe a righteous person? *1 John 3:7*

27. What is our "new self" created to be like according to Paul in Ephesians 4:22-24?

Every Christian has felt the Spirit lead them into doing things, saying things and being things that defy human nature. I remember after experiencing the loss of one of our babies, my doctor asked me how my husband and I were able to hold up so well. The truth is, it was not humanly possible to hold up as we did; our strength came from the Spirit working overtime in our hearts, giving us the peace and comfort we needed. With the aid of the Spirit, we can bite our tongues, love our defiant children, love our enemies, be kind to those who are out to harm us, choose to not retaliate or seek revenge, deny our immoral desires and accept a death in our family. It's not always easy, but rest assured, the Spirit is always there giving us the words, wisdom, understanding, peace, comfort, strength and power that we need to accomplish and accept God's will for us in every situation.

READ: John 16:11

> 28. What is the third aspect of conviction the Spirit works on in us? Who is the prince of this world?
>
> 29. What do these passages in John tell us about the prince of this world?
>
> *John 12:31*
>
> *John 14:30*
>
> *John 16:11*
>
> 30. When was Satan driven out? When was his hold on Jesus released? When did he stand condemned? *Colossians 2:14-15 & Hebrews 2:14*
>
> 31. Why did Jesus appear? Did He do what He set out to do? *1 John 3:7, 8*

While Jesus and his apostles were finishing up the Last Supper, the Jewish leaders and priests were holding a secret conference in another part of Jerusalem. In the black of night, having judged Jesus a blasphemer and deemed Him worthy of death, they waited for their accomplice and informer to arrive. He would guide them to the place where Jesus could be found in order for them to carry out their sinful sentence.

To someone who is unfamiliar with this story it might seem as though Jesus was defeated and Satan had won. Many Jews believed that. But His death proved otherwise. On the cross Jesus proved Satan had absolutely no hold on Him, not even in His darkest hour! Satan was powerless to stop God's plan to save man. Instead, the crucifixion exposed Satan as the weak liar that he is, and it also put into motion the new working of the Holy Spirit in the lives of men.

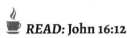
READ: John 16:12

32. Why do you think the apostles were unable to bear what Jesus had to tell them?

Jesus was not able to teach His disciples everything they needed to know in the three short years He was with them. On this memorable evening, just hours before His crucifixion, Jesus had so much more He wanted to tell His apostles. We can hear, see and almost feel the tremendous compassion Jesus had for these men as He tried to explain how they would be receiving a Comforter after He was gone. However, Jesus realized they were unable to take in any more information that night. He then shared some incredibly good news that would change their lives forever.

READ: John 16:13

33. What did Jesus tell the apostles the Spirit would do for them? John 16:13 & *John 14:26*

When the Holy Spirit came in Acts 2, He entered some men in miraculous ways, revealing the truth about Jesus and inspiring them to write the New Testament. We will forevermore know the truth about Jesus, who He is, what He did for us, and all that He will do for those who believe in Him because of these inspired men of God (2 Timothy 3:16; & 2 Peter 1:21).

The Spirit still leads us to truth today. He guides unbelievers who are searching for fulfillment in their lives to a way out of their sinful state and into the arms of their Father. He guides the believer who is seeking God's will in his life or who is studying and searching the Scriptures for truth in a matter. Whatever truth man is searching for, the Spirit is always there to lead him to answers and help him apply them to his life. The Spirit uses whatever means it takes to face us with the truth. It may be a neighbor, a family member, a sermon, a song, a chance meeting, a TV show, a book, a Scripture, a remark that triggers a thought, or an insight while praying and meditating.

When Jesus Speaks, Will You Listen?

*READ:* John 16:13

34. On whose authority does the Spirit speak?

35. According to 1 Corinthians 2:10-12 how does God reveal truth to us?

Jesus tells us that He and the Father are one and that He does nothing by Himself; only following what He sees God doing (John 5:19; 10:30). The heavenly "circle of life" begins with Jesus saying and doing what God said and did, then the Spirit repeating and doing what Jesus said and did. And then we in turn, saying and doing what the Spirit teaches us to say and do. It is comforting to know that when we are convicted, inspired or enlightened, it has come from the Spirit who has searched heaven for the answer to give us. He only tells us what the Father instructs Him to tell us. We will never be led astray when we listen and obey the Spirit's teaching.

*READ:* John 16:13-14

36. What will the Spirit tell the apostles and what will He do for them?

Jesus promised the apostles that the Counselor would explain to them the things that would transpire in the future. Jesus was not speaking of psychic powers as we think of them today, but of a divine understanding of His return, of judgment, and the kingdom yet to come.

As we read the New Testament, we have proof in our hands of the Spirit coming and doing that very thing. We are told reassuringly that Jesus will return, of the immediate judgment that will follow, and the blissful home that awaits those who are faithful.

37. Who does Paul say is able to reveal the mystery of Christ? *Ephesians 3:4-5*

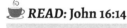*READ:* John 16:14

38. How will the Spirit bring glory to Christ?

Again, we have a chain of command: the Spirit glorifies the Son, as the Son glorifies the Father.

39. Read John 5:19-20 and explain what Jesus does.

Jesus assures us that the Spirit has only one motivation: to bring glory to Jesus. The Spirit does that by revealing all the things Jesus wants Him to reveal and to whom Jesus wants the Spirit to reveal them. When the Spirit convicts us of our sins, He brings glory to Jesus; when He leads us to truth, He brings glory to Jesus; when He comforts us and encourages us and teaches us in the millions of ways He does, He brings glory to Jesus. His job is to bring Christ to life in our hearts, minds and lives. When He does—you got it—He brings glory to Jesus.

40. How does the Spirit take what is Jesus' and make it known to us? *John 16:14-15*

As the Spirit sees our needs, He goes to the Lord for answers and communicates them to us in various ways.

Jesus is very emphatic that we understand exactly where the Spirit is getting His answers. What a comfort it is to know that the Spirit and Christ and our Father are all working together for our salvation.

READ: John 16:15

41. From whom does Jesus get His information?

I remember as a teenager hearing a preacher ask the question, "If the Holy Spirit died today, would your life be any different?" I remember being stumped. At that time I didn't have a definitive answer for that question. Many years later I, like you, have come to rely on the Spirit so much I couldn't live without Him for even a day. I certainly could not write this lesson without first praying for the Spirit's guidance to lead my thoughts.

Without the Spirit, we could never grow up spiritually. We'd be like a baby who tried to raise herself. She'd never figure out right from wrong, nor how to share because she'd be too determined with getting her own way.

Because of the Holy Spirit, we have a desire to give ourselves over to God's will. He helps us overcome our selfish, human desires, making us pure and sinless in our Father's eyes. We can live righteous, holy lives that are full of blessings, love, joy and comfort only because of the Spirit's influence in us.

What an overwhelming and undeserved blessing our Father has given us in His gift of the Holy Spirit. How very blessed we are because Jesus left this earth a long time ago and sent us a Comforter.

> *"I tell you the truth: it is for your good that I am going away . . . Unless I go away, the Counselor will not come to you." John 16:7*

ꙮ Becoming a Servant ꙮ — Lesson Six

"I tell you the truth, no servant is greater than his master …" –John 13:16

How many of us would say we just love being a servant to others? We could serve others and do menial jobs all day long and love every minute of it! I think it is safe to say not many of us love serving others, especially not as much as when we are served by someone else. We tend to have a little selfish DNA in us that most of the time resists putting others' needs before our own.

In our study today, Jesus will teach a lesson through His example that will make us blush when we think of our true heart's description of servanthood. As Jesus' Galilean ministry is coming to an end, it is apparent His apostles, these great men of faith, are still thinking like worldly men when it comes to serving others. We see this in many passages as we hear the twelve discussing who is the greatest and who will sit on the earthly throne next to Jesus. Of course to their defense, they mistakenly think Jesus is going to set up an earthly kingdom. They think this to the very end of Jesus' life.

During His time with the apostles, Jesus spoke about the importance of being a servant and putting others first, but somehow, the apostles never understood it to mean *they* needed to serve others. They saw themselves as an elite group of men, which made them blind to the fact they had become arrogant, self-centered and prideful. They could not see that they were on the verge of becoming absolutely useless to Jesus and His real kingdom.

Our lesson begins in an upper room in Jerusalem. The apostles and Jesus are sharing their last Passover meal together. It will be the last few hours the twelve will see Jesus alive. A monumental evening to say the least. We are so privileged to have such a detailed account of what Jesus said and did with His apostles in those final hours. (It makes me wonder what I might choose to talk about to my family and close friends in my final hours.) Among other things, He taught a lesson on the importance of serving others. This is an important lesson for the apostles for so many reasons: for the success of the new church, for the influence they will have as they teach others and for spreading the gospel globally. These men had to have a different worldview of servanthood and the role they would play in establishing the new church.

I want you to imagine with me, sitting in the upper room during this Passover meal. Sit yourself close enough to overhear Jesus talking to our brothers, witness first hand His outrageous behavior, and observe their humble – and not so humble, response.

Before we begin, read the whole account in John 13:1-17.

READ: John 13:1

1. What does this passage tell us Jesus knew of his days on earth?

Every year Jews from all over the world came to Jerusalem for the Passover celebration. Depending on the commentary you read, anywhere from 250,000 to well over a 1,000,000 Jews would crowd into Jerusalem. If they could, they would stay through Pentecost, which was 50 days after Passover. Jerusalem was bursting with visitors making their annual pilgrimage for this festival. To help accommodate this influx, Jews living in Jerusalem would open their homes and welcome out-of-town family and friends needing lodging, as all the public housing would be full to capacity.

2. In Mark 8:31-32, 9:30-32 and 10:32-34, what did Jesus tell His disciples about Himself as they made the journey to Jerusalem?

3. Why had Jesus come into this world? *John 12:27-28*

READ: John 13:2

At the beginning of this Passover meal everything is going along as any other Passover meal for Jesus and our brothers. But sometime during the meal while everyone is still reclining and eating, Jesus gets up from the table.

But, before we get to the crux of the lesson Jesus is about to teach, John tells us Satan had put it in the heart of Judas to betray Jesus. Satan was with Judas every step of the way as he made his dreadful arrangement with the Jewish leaders to find a quiet place in which to hand Jesus over to be arrested. The 30 pieces of silver must still be rattling in his money pouch. Let's take a small detour from the meal and examine the weakness and temptation of Judas.

4. What was Judas' job as an apostle? How do you think it affected him? *John 12:4-6*

5. Explain what was happening to the disciples in John 6:53, 60-66. Do you think this could have influenced Judas? Why or why not?

6. Do you believe Judas' fate was sealed, or did he have a choice? *John 6:70-71*

7. When did Satan enter Judas? What do you think is the difference in prompting Judas and entering him? *John 13:2, 26-27*

Just as Satan tempted Judas, using his own greedy desires, he tempts us today. Satan will not bother to tempt us with something we have no interest in. He loves to prey upon our weaknesses and whisper sweet-sounding rationalizations in our minds. How it makes him smile to see us fall for it. When he can sway us to give in to our desires, turn a deaf ear to our faith and deny our love for God, oh, how that makes his day. And oh, the damage he can cause to our eternal souls.

Satan is keenly aware of each and every weakness we have! At times Satan may be more in tuned to what tempts us than we are. When we lose sight of what tempts us or rationalize away their seriousness, Satan gains a huge advantage. But when we are honest and realistic about our weaknesses, it takes away Satan's power over us. That is why putting on the full armor of God is so vital to a believer (Ephesians 6:10-20).

One of the best ways to avoid and overcome temptation is to give serious thought, truly pinpoint exactly when, where, why and how we personally are tempted. Your temptation may come at work while you are with co-workers, or at home late at night on the Internet, or when you are alone with a particular person, or in a certain kind of establishment or situation. It may come from the books you choose to read or movies you view. The most important aspect of the whole temptation process boils down to us being wise enough to recognize Satan at work in us. Judas didn't seem to have a clue he was being manipulated by Satan.

8. How does God help us resist Satan's tempting arrows? *1 Corinthians 10:13*

What a difference it would have been for Judas had he sought a way to resist Satan.

When Jesus Speaks, Will You Listen?

9. What is the most effective way you have found to avoid temptation?

It is with sad hearts that we return to the upper room. Knowing how this will ultimately destroy Judas makes what is about to take place even more tragic.

READ: John 13:3-4

10. The word "so" is used in a way that would mean that is why Jesus got up. Why do you think Jesus got up from the meal and began washing the apostles' feet?

11. For an example of what can happen to a group of believers who suffer from hero worship, read 1 Corinthians 1:10-12. What do we find our brothers and sisters arguing over?

Jesus knew He was about to leave the world and place the responsibility of establishing a new church to these men. If they had not learned to put their egos aside and serve others, the church could have been divided twelve different ways as they all worked to have the biggest and best church.

If this can happen to a church when the traveling preachers have moved on, just think of the damage that could be done to a church if it were the local church leaders promoting this kind of adoration. Paul quickly taught our Corinthian brothers and sisters to remain united and to remember who had died for them. Paul did not want any part of hero worship (*1 Corinthians 1:10:13*).

READ: John 13:4-5

12. Describe what Jesus did next. As you do, realize you are describing the dutiful act of a slave as he serves his master's guests.

Washing feet was considered a humiliating, menial task. One that Jewish slaves were relieved from having to perform. Yet, Jesus, unpretentiously made a spectacle of himself before the apostles. He wanted to impress upon them the absolute essentiality for them to lose their enormous ego and pride and to understand the significance and value in serving others.

13. How important was status, rank and ego to Jesus? *Philippians 2:6-8 & Matthew 20:28*

Because the apostles were reclining at the table, it was easy for Jesus to get to their feet. Imagine what it must have been like when Jesus stopped to wash the feet of Judas. Perhaps He even began with Judas in order to give him one more chance to change his mind. Each of the apostles in turn allowed Jesus to wash their feet. Though they were horrified by His behavior and for the shame and humiliation He was bringing on Himself, they kept silent—until He came to Peter.

**READ: John 13:6**

14. What did Peter do when Jesus tried to wash his feet? Why?

Peter was always acting first and asking questions later. On this evening it is a real weakness of his. He should have taken lessons from the other apostles and quietly waited for Jesus to explain Himself.

But no, Peter kicked his feet out of the water and refused to allow Jesus to wash them. Not because he felt unworthy to have his feet washed by Jesus mind you, nor did Peter think he should be the one washing the feet of Jesus. No, no, no, Peter's problem with it was that he saw Jesus doing the work of a servant, a common slave, when He should be acting like a king! Peter had a "we pay people to do that" kind of attitude. This refusal of Peter's is an illumination into his heart, exposing a man who is not ready to serve others. Washing the feet of the apostles was as culturally taboo in Jesus' day as it would be for a bride or groom to prepare, serve and clean up dishes at their own wedding today. Peter would never have humiliated himself like that, and he was not about to allow Jesus to do it either.

READ: John 13:7-8

In order to make him understand, Jesus tested Peter's pride and his humiliation. But even after a short explanation and rebuke, Peter still refused to allow Jesus to wash his feet. A false sense of self-worth was so ingrained in Peter's mind that he could not see where Jesus was going with His example that night.

Knowing the hearts of these men as Jesus did, He understood this lesson would take them time to think through. For one to willingly give up status was culturally and politically incorrect in their eyes. It was seen as a weakness, plain and simple. It would also take them time to fully understand their place in the new kingdom.

When Jesus Speaks, Will You Listen?

Even though Jesus mentioned three times on their way to Jerusalem that He was going to die, they never understood that His death would mean He would not reign on an earthly throne. I know what you're thinking, but this thought of an earthly kingdom ran deep in their Jewish heritage. Jesus knew this was very confusing to them and He explained that they would understand later.

The apostles needed some time to process this new way of thinking regarding serving others, much like one who is in shock over an unexpected tragedy. The apostles needed time for the fact to sink in that they would not have a place of prominence on earth, and that they were going to become servants not lords. Not exactly what they signed up for, they might be thinking right about now.

> **15. When do you think the apostles understood the full implications of Jesus' example of serving others?**

**READ:** John 13:8

> **16. What is it about the statement of Jesus to Peter, "Unless I wash you, you have no part with Me," that brought Peter to his senses?**

Jesus was trying to get Peter to submit to His will even though Peter did not fully understand it. This can be the strongest test of anyone's faith. Abraham gave us a wonderful example of blind obedience.

> **17. What do we learn from Abraham in Hebrews 11:8?**

> **18. Do you ever have trouble submitting to the Lord when you don't understand why something is happening? How does that compare with Peter's attitude that night in the Upper Room? Try to think of a specific situation.**

READ: John 13:9-10

19. Explain how Peter was useless to Jesus if he did not allow Him to wash his feet?

20. What did Jesus say in answer to Peter's request?

Can you picture a little hidden smile on the face of Jesus as He heard Peter's answer? Now he is giving Jesus permission to give him a complete bath! The smile of Jesus was probably like that of a teacher when a student finally grasps a difficult concept. But His smile quickly fades as He observes another student, one who would not catch on, whose conscience must have been burning with guilt as he listened to the conversation between Jesus and Peter.

21. To whom was Jesus referring as "not clean"?

READ: John 13:11

22. What part of Judas was not clean?

Judas sat and ate the Passover meal with the other apostles and discussed along with the others who was the greatest. He probably allowed Jesus to wash his feet, watched and listened to the interchange of Jesus and Peter and heard Jesus tell Peter He could not have anything to do with him if he would not submit and allow Him to wash his feet. What he must have thought when he heard Jesus say, "Not all of you are clean." No, what Judas seemed to be concentrating on that night was the 30 pieces of silver (the price of a slave) that he had received just a little while ago. Nothing that happened that evening seemed to touch his dark, black heart. Although Judas' feet were washed, he still was not clean.

23. Is it possible for one to be washed, but not clean today? Explain.

When Jesus Speaks, Will You Listen?

24. What was the difference between Peter and Judas that night that made one repent and the other sit quietly, unaffected and unrepentant?

25. How was Peter tempted that night? Are we tempted in the same way today? Explain your answer.

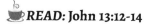
READ: John 13:12-14

26. In setting the stage for his explanation, who did Jesus say He was?

When Jesus finished washing feet, He put down the basin of water, took off the wet, dirty towel from around his waist, and put his outer clothing back on. He walked back to the table and reclined with the apostles. Can't you just feel all eyes on Him as they tried to understand what had just happened and what in the world Jesus was getting at? Getting to the heart of what Jesus wanted to convey, He first asked them a question: "Do you understand what I have done for you?" His question seemed to puzzle them. Or perhaps it was a rhetorical question. At any rate, you can feel the quiet in the room. No one willing to even hazard a guess. The hearts of this band of brothers were pounding in anticipation as they anxiously awaited an explanation from their Lord and Teacher.

27. Explain the point Jesus was making as the Lord and Teacher washed their feet.

In the first half of John's book, Jesus is referred to more as Teacher. In the second half, He is referred to more as Lord. This demonstrates the spiritual growth of His disciples.

Jesus begins as our Teacher also, giving us rules and teaching us how to live by them. Eventually

He slips out of teacher mode in our minds and becomes Lord and Savior of our hearts, the One who has authority over us and the power to save our souls.

READ: John 13:15

28. Jesus said He had set them an example. What is it Jesus expects them to do?

It is important to realize that Jesus was not instituting a new ritual of foot washing, but rather He was exemplifying the humble attitude required of a believer. When you really think about it, was there any other way Jesus could have made these men see this lesson than for He, their Messiah, willingly humbling Himself in order to serve them? And can He make it any clearer for you and me that there really is no task too lowly for us to do in the kingdom?

29. What was the Apostle Paul's philosophy on serving others? *I Corinthians 9:22-23*

30. Washing others' feet is translated into serving others even when the task seems menial or lowly. This includes not looking the other way when someone needs help. According to these Scriptures, whom are we to serve and what are we to do for them?

Matthew 5:42

Luke 6:27

John 13:34-35

Romans 14:1-3

When Jesus Speaks, Will You Listen?

Galatians 6:1-2

1 Peter 4:9

If we are really honest with ourselves, we must admit, we dodge menial tasks at work, at home or in our neighborhoods whenever we can. How long will a piece of paper lie between your home and your neighbors', with each waiting for the other to pick it up? How long will the 2 & 3 year old class go without a teacher? This is the type of attitude Jesus was trying to get the apostles to change. If the church was to survive, these men had to learn to get over their egotistical false sense of self-worth and be willing to do whatever is needed no matter the task. Their focus on this earth needed to be the kingdom, not their self-worth or position in it.

It is human nature to be self-centered. It's the one gene we all share, but this attitude can destroy a church as well as a family.

READ: John 13:16

31. Identify the servant and the master in verse 16.

32. Write the point Jesus was making in verse 16 in your own words.

Jesus had a point to make from the beginning of dinner and He finally gets to the heart of the matter. Though the apostles do not understand completely what Jesus is doing and exactly what He means, they do know this is a monumental evening. One thing these men do understand without any doubt, is that Jesus is greater than they are. There is a unanimous agreement about that. As they put the evening's events all together, they must grapple with their attitudes, learn some true humility and grasp the whole idea that everyone, including themselves, has the responsibility to serve others.

33. What lesson can we learn from verse 16 today?

This is a tremendous concept we must all take to heart. Learning to see the ultimate good in serving others and volunteering to do even menial tasks is a test we face every day. As we observe the example of Jesus, and understand the apostles' resistance, comparing them to our own, and as we acknowledge the fact that it is not easy to have a servant's heart, it helps us put our fanciful view of ourselves in proper perspective. When we see how important this lesson is to Jesus, and knowing how vital it is that we learn it, is very convicting. The early church and the church today cannot grow, thrive, or be blessed if its members do not serve each other humbly. There is no room for egos in the church.

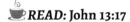*READ:* John 13:17

34. What did Jesus tell the apostles would be the result if they humbled themselves and served one another?

35. Name some acts of service we can humbly do for others.

36. How are we blessed when we do serve others?

We are all going to have trouble with keeping our selfish nature in check from time to time. But with a desirous heart, we can become the servants God created us to be, the humble servant Jesus exemplified that evening in the upper room with His apostles.

When Jesus Speaks, Will You Listen?

So, next time you have the opportunity to serve someone, cast your inflated ego aside and remember these words of Jesus.

"I tell you the truth, no servant (us) is greater than his master (Jesus), nor is a messenger (us again) greater than the one who sent him (Jesus). Now that you know these things, (Sweetheart,) you will be blessed if you do them." John 13:16-17

Hypocrisy — Lesson Seven

"... I tell you the truth, they have received their reward in full." –Matthew 6:5

During Jesus' three-year ministry, He taught many lessons on the importance of a genuine faith and the dangers of hypocrisy. But the religious leaders, and even His chosen apostles seemed to be clueless when it came to judging their motives for doing good things. This idea actually sounded ridiculous to them, but Jesus persistently taught the importance of a man's heart. He taught that a pure heart was more important than the act of kindness itself. This concept was a giant leap in the thinking of most Jews. In fact, they had been taught by the example of the Jewish leaders how to perfect the art of flaunting one's acts of righteousness in front of the biggest and most important audience possible.

Jesus spoke very plainly about hypocrisy, especially to the Pharisees. And WOE, did they ever get His point. The Pharisees, apostles and followers of Jesus knew and practiced the Old Law on a daily basis. They knew when to fast, when to pray and when to give alms. But to do these things and get no attention or praise was inconceivable. What was the point if no one saw? I can just imagine the looks on their faces when Jesus told them to stop exploiting themselves and to do their good deeds in secret if they wanted to receive a reward for doing them.

In today's lesson, we will see how essential it is to have a pure heart as we go about our everyday lives. It is not enough to simply do the right thing; one must have the right motive for doing it. I want to warn you up front that hypocrisy is insidious and very difficult to recognize in oneself. This lesson will call us to be painfully honest as we search our hearts for motives.

READ: Matthew 6:1-8

Notice Jesus did not give His listeners a definition of a righteous act. It wasn't necessary because all Jews knew very well what a righteous act was. Jesus had witnessed Jews performing the very acts for which He was about to chastise them in the market places, on street corners and at banquets. He had observed them giving alms in the temple and synagogues with trumpets blasting. He saw the spectacles they made of themselves as they prayed in public and how they would try to look like death warmed over when they fasted.

One important point to watch for in this lesson is how serious Jesus is as He warns of the dangers of hypocrisy and how easily it can creep into one's heart.

READ: Matthew 6:1 again

When Jesus Speaks, Will You Listen?

1. What is Jesus warning His followers *not* to do?

2. What does Jesus say to do in Matthew 5:16?

At first glance this can look like Jesus was trying to have it both ways. But in Chapter 5, Jesus was encouraging His followers to perform righteous deeds in the open so that others would see them and praise their Heavenly Father. However, some were seeking praise for themselves when they performed their righteous acts. Can you imagine that!

It's one thing to help a poor neighbor so that Mrs. Jones next door will see and want to know a God like the one you serve. It's quite another to help the poor with the hope that Mrs. Jones will be impressed and think *you* are wonderful. Jesus said, "Let your light shine," but He did not mean for us to create a spotlight for ourselves. Jesus is stressing the importance of our heart when we do something for someone. The purpose for which you do anything, the attitude in which you do it, and your motive for doing it is as important, if not more important, than the act itself.

3. What does God think of a person who does their acts of righteousness to be seen by Mrs. Jones?

4. What reward do we cut ourselves off from when we boast of our righteous acts?

Notice again that Jesus did not say if you do righteous deeds, but rather, *when* you do them. His audience understood that they needed to do righteous acts—they had scrolls and scrolls on that subject—but one's motive for doing good was never stressed.

5. Name some righteous acts we do every day that we might be tempted to boast about or do for show. (Continue your notes on the next page).

5. Continued . . .

Any act of righteousness or kind deed that we do in the name of our Lord brings glory and praise to God. When we pray for others, teach others, give to others, help others, invite others to Bible study or church, sing praises, encourage the discouraged, bring someone back to the Lord or do anything for others that exhibits our devotion to God, we bring Him glory and praise *if* it is done with the proper motive and attitude. If we are honest with ourselves, we can see that it is very easy to do the right thing for the wrong reason. And when we do, we receive absolutely no reward from God. One's attitude is everything.

READ: Matthew 6:2-4

6. What is one to do when giving to the needy? How does one do that today?

7. What did the hypocrites do?

8. Why did they announce it like that?

9. What exactly was their reward?

10. What sort of rewards does one seek from men today?

When Jesus Speaks, Will You Listen?

11. What are ways one can give today?

12. How can we give with wrong motives?

13. In verse 3, how did Jesus say they should give? Explain how one can give that secretly.

14. Explain what one learns about giving from Deuteronomy 15:11.

The Jewish nation was the only religion in Jesus' day with an established system that provided for the poor and needy. Because the Jews did heed the Old Law, their poor and needy were taken care of very well. Their temple had six receptacles placed throughout to make it convenient for contributors to give to the poor.

The problem Jesus was addressing was not the issue of giving per se, but rather the attitudes and motives of the one giving. Were they helping others for their own praise, or for the praise and glory of the Lord? That is a good question for us to ask ourselves today. This is the point in which the insidious hypocrisy Jesus is warning us about can creep in. And the consequence is not a cute wink or a soft slap on the wrist.

15. What do these statements of Jesus tell you about motives and attitudes?

   Matthew 15:7-8

   Matthew 23:5-7

Matthew 23:28

16. What does it mean to you that God sees what you have done in secret?

Have you ever felt like the child who huddled under his covers to hide from someone? Blankets can make a child feel like they can't be seen. We can feel that way too, thinking that because we cannot see God, He cannot see us. Or that if no one else saw our unkindness, we escaped unscathed. But rest assured, God does indeed see us when we don't see Him. He knows whether we give in secret or with trumpets (even if the trumpets or praise is only sounding in our minds).

17. When does God reward us for our giving? When is our giving unworthy of God's reward?

18. What does Paul tell us about our deeds and our rewards in these passages?

Ephesians 6:8

Colossians 3:23-24

Part of our trouble with being transparent is that God permits us to receive a reward of praise from our peers if that is what we are seeking. But sadly, that is all we will receive. If it is a reward from God that motivates our act of righteousness, it must be kept secret from everyone. Then God, whose rewards always exceed our accomplishments, will reward us with eternal life! Not a bad trade-off for keeping a secret. Eternal life with God makes earthly rewards of praise and accolades seem very trivial. When put side-by-side, no one would choose the praise of men over eternal life. Yet each time we do something for the recognition, or discreetly leak out information touting our good works, we are making that very choice.

READ: Matthew 6:5-6
The Jews made it a daily habit to pray three times a day: the third, sixth and ninth hours, that is

9:00 AM, 12:00 PM and 3:00 PM. These were their traditional and formal times to pray. But like us, they also prayed during worship in their synagogues and in their homes.

> 19. Who does Jesus warn His followers not to emulate when they pray?
>
> 20. Where did the hypocrites love to pray and why?
>
> 21. Once again for emphasis, what is the reward of the hypocrite who prays for show?

The Jews used their prayer times to gather in a group and pray. Those who lived in Jerusalem would go to the temple to pray, while those outside of town would go to their synagogues. Often men would plan their day to be in the most busy part of town at the 3:00 o'clock prayer time to be seen by more people. They would hurry downtown to the bustling streets of Jerusalem and stop in the city square to pray as loudly as they could. You can imagine the attention they would draw to themselves.

> 22. Note the occasion for a meeting in these passages and note the time of day.
>
>   *Acts 2:1*
>
>   *Acts 3:1*
>
>   *Acts 10:9*
>
> 23. Do you think those who prayed on the street thought God was impressed with their prayers? Explain your answer.

These Jewish men were very religious and never would have done anything they knew was in obvious conflict with the Scriptures. Yet, how they could think that the Almighty God would be impressed with their street corner theatrics is a puzzlement—until I think back to the last time I was asked to lead a prayer in our ladies Bible class. Has the following ever happened to you? You are asked to lead a prayer, and immediately your mind begins to list things you can pray about, to the extent you are not listening anymore to comments around you. Finally, you are called upon, and you begin to pray. If you pronounce everyone's name correctly, remember to include some interesting facts about a class member and manage to go on and on about current events, you sit down feeling pretty good about yourself. You think, "Yeah! I'll probably be asked to lead all the prayers since that was so impressively delivered," and you high five yourself in your mind. I hope this is an exaggeration of how we feel when we pray, but on the other hand... Well, maybe our ancestral brothers and sisters weren't such a puzzlement after all.

Oftentimes we let ourselves off the hook by comparing ourselves literally to those in Jesus' story. We gloss over our heart problem by assuring ourselves that at least we have never stood on a corner and made a spectacle of ourselves. Oh, but glossing over, rationalizing, and denying our true heart's intentions, are all part of concealing our true motives.

Anything we do under public eye has the potential to do one of two things, either bring glory and praise to God, or a pat on our back as we soak in the compliments for ourselves. Only the honest of hearts and God know the truth.

24. Who should be the audience when one prays?

25. What dangers do we face when we pray publicly? How can they be avoided?

At first glance it may seem that Jesus was telling His followers to avoid public prayers, but as we read through the New Testament, we realize this is not the case at all. The early church prayed together all the time.

26. Where did these early Christians meet to pray?

Acts 12:5, 12

Acts 16:13

Acts 21:5

When Jesus Speaks, Will You Listen?

27. Is Jesus speaking literally when He tells us to go in a room and close the door? If not, what did Jesus mean?

28. Look up these Scriptures and note what led Jesus to want to pray alone and where He went to pray.

   Matthew 14:21-23

   Mark 1:35

   Luke 5:15-16

   Luke 6:12

29. What happens when we pray alone that does not happen when we pray publicly?

30. What can happen to our daily prayers offered in secret?

31. What is God's reward for those who pray in secret with a sincere heart?

READ: Matthew 6:7-8

Our heavenly Father longs for us to communicate with Him. Yet, how we communicate with Him is very important. We all love to talk with our children and grandchildren. However, if they were to whine and complain and demand their own way constantly, it would grate on us and we would tire of it quickly, causing us to find ways to stay away from them for a while. It does not make for pleasant conversation, and I believe our whining, complaining and demanding our way can make God feel the same way about us.

I like to picture God in my mind when praying. I try to visualize Him listening to me, which helps me keep my prayer personal without wandering into meaningless rhetoric. I am convinced that we would pray differently if we could see God face-to-face. The fact that He is unseen makes us feel we are praying into thin air at times, or praying without realizing we are literally being heard.

32. How did the pagans pray? Matthew 6:7

33. What does it mean to babble?

34. What did the pagans think they had to do to be heard by their god?

Jesus was not teaching that it was wrong to pray long, meaningful prayers or to repeat yourself when something is distressful and heavy on your heart. This, in fact, is quite the contrary. Let's look at moments in Jesus' life when He was earnestly seeking His Heavenly Father.

35. What do we learn about prayer from Jesus in these passages?

Matthew 26:44

Luke 6:12

Luke 18:1

When Jesus Speaks, Will You Listen?

As we witness the prayer life of Jesus, we see plainly that He was not condemning long or repetitive prayers. Rather, He was warning us against prayers that are not sincere communication with our Heavenly Father, flowing from our heart to His. Hypocrisy happens only when our prayers consist of meaningless words uttered to impress those around us. The content of our prayer is for God; it is to Him that we are talking, not to each other. When we try to gain praise for ourselves while praising God or praying to Him, we have lost our reward with Him.

READ: Matthew 7:1-5

Another form of hypocrisy we may be more familiar with is that of pointing out faults in others while denying our own. This is the proverbial "pot calling the kettle black" syndrome.

36. Describe the mental gymnastics Jesus is revealing in this passage.

37. How do we do this today?

38. Add your name and then read verse 3. Can you think of a time Jesus might have said this to you?

39. What did Jesus say must be done before a person can take the speck out of another's eye? And how does one do that? *Matthew 7:5*

40. What is one trying to accomplish by hiding their big black sin while pointing out a tiny sin in another?

41. Is Jesus saying one should never point out another person's sin? Explain.

42. What do these passages teach us should be our motive for judging others?

> *Leviticus 19:17*

> *James 5:19-20*

As we look closely at Jesus' parable in Matthew 7, we see that He is talking more about hypocrisy than He is about judging others. When we are in the grips of sin, we are not in a position to correct anyone. We must first get our own life right, and only then, will we have the sound judgment to discern what Moses and Jesus' brother James tell us we should do. Finding fault in others while ignoring or rationalizing our own faults is a very common form of hypocrisy today.

READ: Matthew 23:23-26, 33

43. What was Jesus' mood and tone as He spoke to the Pharisees?

44. In verse 23 what did the Pharisees do right?

45. Name the 3 things they had neglected.

Now there is something we, like the apostles, didn't see coming. There is a terrible punishment for those of us who do not get our egos in check and who do not think anything of taking away God's glory for our own pat on the back.

> **46. What is to be the fate of those of us who are hypocritical?**
>
> *Matthew 23:33*
>
>
> *Matthew 24:51*

Hypocrisy is an ugly thing; just talking about it certainly gets Jesus upset. Who among us wouldn't want to sneak out of the presence of Jesus as He hits the Pharisees with woe after woe, exposing their hypocrisy. Yet, on the other hand, we are blessed to have this lesson from Jesus. Without it, we would all join our ancient brothers and sisters, as well as the world, and go through life praising ourselves and thinking nothing of it.

To realize God knows our innermost thoughts and motives should stop us in our tracks and cause us to examine our hearts. God rewards the pure in heart, those who do good things to glorify Him. Jesus says the pure in heart will see God (Matthew 5:8). Did you hear that—WILL SEE GOD! Honestly, can you think of a greater blessing or reward?

As we examine our hearts for purity, let's listen one more time to our Lord and Savior as He warns us to be honest with ourselves knowing the grave consequences that are at stake.

". . . I tell you the truth, they have received their reward in full."

Whose reward are you seeking?

 Anger   Lesson Eight

"But I tell you that anyone who is angry with his brother will be subject to judgment . . ."
–Matthew 5:22

In preparing for this lesson I am amazed how much the Bible, and Jesus in particular, has to say about anger. The Ecclesiastes writer is right, there is nothing new under the sun. We humans have been having trouble controlling our anger since time began.

In the time of Jesus, it was well understood that murder was illegal and sinful, but anger was not considered wrong. In fact, nothing of motives, attitudes, or one's heart was ever considered an issue to a Jew. So, when Jesus teaches this lesson, it sounds very alien to His followers. It is more than some folks are able to accept, especially the leaders and teachers of the Law.

One sunny day when Jesus had a huge crowd of people following Him, He went up on a mountainside and sat down with them. When they were settled and seated comfortably, He began to teach them. The Sermon on the Mount is very familiar to most of us, we may even have some of it memorized. But when Jesus first spoke these words, it was difficult for His disciples to grasp this unheard of concept because the idea was unlike anything they had ever been taught. This lesson is going to require more than just obeying the letter of the Law. It will force His audience, you and me, to realize our behavior, attitudes, thoughts and motives are what God is looking at rather than our adherence to the Law.

So grab a sweater and that picnic quilt, and let's go to the mountain to listen in as Jesus teaches His disciples.

READ: Matthew 5:21-26

1. Who was Jesus' audience on the mountain? *Matthew 5:1*

2. To which of the commandments was Jesus referring in verse 21? *Exodus 20:13*

When Jesus Speaks, Will You Listen?

3. What do we learn about murder and its judgment from reading Genesis 9:6 and Numbers 35:30?

The judgment Jesus is referring to in verse 21 is a limited, earthly judgment for the crime of murder. It is a death sentence handed down by the court system. Of course this judgment is based on the original 10 Commandments given by God to Moses. But the Law had been added to so often it was hardly recognizable as the original Law of Moses. One obvious deviance in the Jewish judicial system, as it was upheld in the day of Jesus, was that it did not take into consideration the intent of the Law. What the guilty party did was on trial, but not his heart. It might clear a man of murder, but it did not deal with the sin of anger, hate and vengeance.

READ: Matthew 5:22

Jesus wisely quoted from the Old Law throughout His ministry knowing that if there was one thing His Jewish audience knew well, it was the Law of Moses. They had heard the books of Law read by priests in their synagogues since the time they were born. In addition to the Law being read in public, it was also taught in the home and in school. However, over the centuries the scribes, Pharisees and teachers of the Law would re-interpret the Old Law by combining their own traditions and rules as additions. They would redefine words in order to create loopholes that would allow a person to do just about anything they wanted to without actually breaking the letter of the Law. They were masters at it.

Jesus, of course, also knew the Law of Moses! On this day, He wanted His followers to understand two things: 1) He had the authority to challenge the additional writings and teachings of the Law; 2) There was a difference between obeying the letter of the Law and actually letting the Law change one's heart, mind, attitude, motive and behavior.

4. What does Matthew 5:17 say Jesus had come to earth to do? What had He not come to do?

Jesus was not changing the Law of Moses, but rather He was emphasizing the intent of it. The Jewish leaders had twisted the Law so badly at times their rendition was exactly opposite of what God intended. These traditions became the law. They had been taught, practiced and handed down from generation to generation for so long, the leaders and common Jews alike didn't realize it had been skewed. Jesus, *knowing* the Scribes and Pharisees were incapable of interpreting the Law accurately, challenged their authority on many occasions. This challenge was seen as a major rebellion and act of insubordination, and even blasphemy, by the leaders. By exposing their limited understanding of the Law, the Law as God intended it to be, Jesus challenged their authority to be teachers of it.

5. Going back a verse, what do you think the Pharisees and teachers of the Law thought of Jesus' comment about them in Matthew 5:20?

Jesus taught with authority because He was authority. He was God incarnate. It was obvious to the crowd that Jesus was not teaching like their own rabbis. Jesus, being divine, knew the truth and He knew the hearts of the Jewish leaders. When Jesus spoke, there was no debating His words. His words and teachings were final, unlike the scribes and Pharisees who would debate a teaching for years. He was not arguing His opinion as the Jewish teachers did. He was simply telling the crowd of listeners the truth as it came from God.

Some listeners didn't like Jesus messing with their laws. But thankfully, others were spellbound and excited that someone would stand up and actually defy their leaders as Jesus did. They loved this new teaching, this new interpretation of the Old Law! Jumping ahead, let's look at how this teaching affected most of His hearers.

6. Describe the people's reaction at the end of Jesus' Sermon on the Mount. Why did they have this reaction? *Matthew 7:28-29*

Before we leave this issue, let's look at one example of the Law in which the scribes and teachers of the Law re-wrote the Law to suit their own best interests. We'll look at a law concerning vows and oaths. It is a great example of the modifications made by the Pharisees and scribes. Then we'll look at what Jesus had to say on that same issue. Remember Jesus was teaching from the Old Law, so He was not introducing anything new. His audience was very familiar with what He was teaching. They were not scratching their heads and asking, "What law?" He was using their old, familiar book of Law.

When Jesus Speaks, Will You Listen?

7. Read these passages and note what was said in the Old Law about making vows and oaths.

>   *Leviticus 19:12*

>   *Numbers 30:2*

8. Now read Matthew 23:16-17 and note the loopholes scribes and Pharisees added.

9. Read Matthew 5:33-37. What did Jesus teach concerning vows? Whose teaching was a more accurate interpretation of the Old Law?

Though Matthew did not record the reaction of the Pharisees and scribes in Matthew 5, we can find other occasions when their reaction is recorded after Jesus challenged their authority.

10. What was the reaction of the Jewish leaders to the teachings of Jesus in these passages.

>   *Matthew 15:12*

>   *Matthew 21:14-15*

>   *Mark 11:18*

>   *Mark 12:12*

Keeping in mind the hearts of some people in Jesus' audience, let's look a little further to and find out what else Jesus has to say about anger.

11. What was the major difference between the way Jesus interpreted the sixth commandment and the way the teachers of the Law interpreted it?

READ: Matthew 5:22

12. What did Jesus say was the punishment for using a very familiar Aramaic word, "Raca," against a brother?

13. Using a Bible dictionary, define the word "Raca."

14. What was the punishment for calling a brother "You fool"?

Jesus' point was not only that His disciples should refrain from using the words 'Raca' and 'You fool' when they were angry — even Jesus did that (Luke 24:25). Doing so would be introducing legalism all over again. His point was that what one thinks about another person in their heart and how they treat that person is as important as obeying the letter of the Law. So, in other words, when we are angry with our brother, it is every bit as serious of an offense as murdering him. Seriously!

15. What did Jesus mean by the phrase, "will be in danger of the fire of hell"?

The punishment passed down by the Jewish court for murder was a death sentence ordered by the civil magistrate. In contrast, Jesus points out that God's punishment for that same person just being angry was eternal damnation in hell! This statement is pretty hard to gloss over, isn't it? Jesus was crystal clear in what He was saying. The court's death penalty was nothing compared to God's eternal penalty for just being angry toward someone. This teaching had to have caused the scribes, Pharisees and rabbis to take pause. After all, it was their job to teach the Law and interpret it! I imagine the question, "Who is this man?" must have been running through the minds of the whole crowd.

16. **What three methods of punishment did Jesus use in His illustrations in verse 22?**

    1.   2.   3.

Everyone on the mountain in Jesus' hearing that day understood the ramifications of the law concerning murder. But most likely, no one had thought about losing one's temper as being a problem.

Some translations read, "But I tell you, that anyone who is angry with his brother *without cause* will be subject to judgment." Whether or not this is a more accurate translation is debatable, but it does bring up an important subject: righteous anger. When is anger justified, and when is it wrong?

17. **What do these passages tell us about anger? Also note who is angry.**

    Psalms 7:11

    Mark 3:5

    Ephesians 4:26-27

18. **Explain what Paul means in Ephesians 4:26.**

19. In your own words, explain when it is appropriate to be angry and when it is not.

20. Make a list of 5 things that make one angry that are not righteous anger. Then make a list of 5 things that are righteous anger. (This is not as easy as you might think.)

Unrighteous Anger	*Righteous Anger*
1.	1.
2.	2.
3.	3.
4.	4.
5.	5.

21. What are some sins we commit while angry? Think long and hard on your answer.

Jesus is not speaking of momentary bursts of frustration we might have when we spill coffee on our white dress, or the baby wakes up five times in the night, or the pay check doesn't go far enough. He is describing what we do *while* we are frustrated and angry. Do we shrug our shoulders and go on, or do we scream obscenities at the coffee, pat the baby a little too hard, or yell and blame our spouse for our problems? It is what we do while we are angry that is important. This is the issue and the heart of our lesson.

Anger is an emotion, and therefore, we cannot simply wish it away (Don't you wish we could?) Many of us try to rationalize or minimize the things we do in anger, especially those who have a problem controlling their temper. Things always seem to be the other person's fault: "If they hadn't made me angry, I would never have _____." God is not blind nor is He deaf. He knows the intention of our hearts. He hears every word we utter (or scream) and sees everything we do while we are angry (Matthew 12:36). It might be someone else's fault you are angry, but it is NEVER their fault that you react in sinful ways. If it is your habit to blame others for your bad temper and your outbursts of anger, understand this behavior is what Jesus is addressing in this passage.

22. List the five things Paul tells us to put aside in Colossians 3:5-7.

Jesus was not talking to His disciples about righteous anger. He was talking about the anger we feel when we are proven wrong and our pride gets injured, when someone terribly inconveniences us, cheats us or hurts our feelings, or when someone goes toe-to-toe with us and defies our will. Jesus said what we do while angry is what is important. Then He put that sinful angry act in perspective by comparing it to murder and giving it the same punishment!

We have all been angry at one time or another. Some of us are better at controlling our anger than others. But it is when we lose our tempers, retaliate or sin in any way while angry, that Jesus is talking about. As an illustration of how anger turns to sin, let's say your neighbor parks his huge dirty monster truck in front of your house day, after day, after day. Finally, you have had enough and confront him, kindly asking him to not park there because you need the space and he has plenty of room in front of his own house. He very rudely swears at you and then slams his door in your face! So, you compose yourself and quietly walk home, trying to overlook his cruelty. The next day he parks in front of your house again. Though you are fuming, you don't do anything right then. Instead, you set your alarm and rise at 3:00 AM, get out your trusty pink baseball bat and bash in his car windshield. Then you return to bed with a satisfied smile on your face.

23. Where did you go wrong? When did anger become sinful?

When we give into our anger and act out our evil thoughts and retaliate, if we are either verbally or physically abusive, spread lies, gossip or slander against someone; we are in a terrible place. Our fate is like a man on death row (danger of hell fire). If we die in this state, without seeking reconciliation, we are doomed. But if we do what Jesus tells us to do next, we can make things right and avoid the eternal punishment for our actions.

This next portion of Scripture is a parable. Here, Jesus explains in practical terms how one can escape eternal damnation and become pure in the sight of God again. In doing so, Jesus again emphasizes how seriously God judges anger.

 **READ:** Matthew 5:23

24. Describe the scenario Jesus has painted for us in verse 23. What is the worshiper about to do and what does he remember?

25. What does one do today that is like the Jews offering a gift at the altar?

In Jesus' parable, the worshiper has sinned against someone. He has bashed in someone's windshield (so to speak). And now with all this on his conscience, he is preparing to worship God by sacrificing an animal on the altar.

Has this ever happened to you, while sitting in a worship service you begin to think about a dispute, fight or a yelling match you had with someone. Maybe you thought of your neighbor's bashed-in windshield?

Jesus is saying that it is a waste of our time to try and worship our loving and forgiving God when we have sinned against someone while angry. His instruction to those who find themselves in this predicament is to clear it up ASAP! Do not even wait for the final "Amen." If you are angry with someone and have sinned against them in anyway, whether it be verbal or physical, you must be reconciled with that person as soon as you can. Meanwhile, don't bother coming to church services.

26. God has always demanded purity of heart from His worshipers. Briefly describe what God says about worship in these Old Testament passages.

Psalm 24:3-4

Jeremiah 7:8-11

Amos 5:21-23

When Jesus Speaks, Will You Listen?

READ: Matthew 5:24

27. What does Jesus say one should do when they find themselves in a sinful situation because of their anger? What should one do today? This sin can be against a child, adult, friend or foe.

Jesus is telling us it is wrong to have angry feelings and unkind thoughts towards another person if we act on them. Letting anger get out of control is to murder someone in our hearts. When we are in this state, our worship is repulsive to our Father and our prayers are not heard(Psalm 66:18). We may as well leave the worship service because our acts of worship are in vain.

28. What does Paul say about worshiping while we are angry or unreconciled?

Ephesians 4:31-32

1 Timothy 2:8

29. What command does John say God gives us in 1 John 4:20-21?

If we want our worship to be acceptable and pleasing to God, we must be at peace with one another having been reconciled and forgiven for each and every outburst of sin we committed while angry. This is a very sobering thought. Apologizing to my neighbor for bashing in his windshield is embarrassing, humiliating and expensive. Ignoring it, since he doesn't go to church anyway (hopefully he doesn't!) is the easiest thing to do. Oh, how we want to rationalize ourselves free of the obligation of admitting we are wrong. How we long to place the blame on someone else's behavior and escape any swallowing of pride or humiliating reconciliation. This can happen in our families, and it probably does more than any other place.

30. What did Jesus teach about forgiveness in these passages?

Matthew 6:14-15

Matthew 18:21-22

Mark 11:25

Jesus' teaching made his audience think long and hard about their behavior. It should make you and me take pause as well. If we have sinned in our anger, we must do something about it. If someone asks us to forgive them, we must forgive them. Ignoring uncomfortable situations for whatever our rationale will only bring hurt and condemnation upon ourselves in the end.

In these next two verses Jesus explains how to turn back to God. They explain what one has to do after they leave the worship service in order to be right with God.

READ: Matthew 5:25

31. Who is the judge in Jesus' story?

32. What is the man in the story encouraged to do?

33. What is the goal for the one settling matters quickly?

34. When a person sins and bashes in their neighbor's windshield, what should be the desire of their heart?

This can be a very difficult step to follow. Our pride is usually very resistant to admitting we had any fault in getting angry. We must remember our eternity depends on whether or not we are honest with ourselves. Let's not be like the Pharisees and make loopholes for ourselves.

In Jesus' parable, He likened the person who sins while he is angry to a man who is on his way to court where he will be tried and sentenced. Jesus said the man should stop, go back and do all he can to clear things up with the person he wronged before it goes to court. If not, the angry outbursts will convict him when he stands before the Judge, the Judge being God.

35. What is the urgency for those who have wronged someone?

36. Just to be clear, what will happen if a person happens to die without ever trying to reconcile?

37. Make a list of things that make you sin in your anger. Then write out ways you can either avoid or control these situations. This is going to be painful, but it could save your soul. Truly.

READ: Matthew 5:26
Jesus continued His parable with the sentencing of the criminal who did not make the needed restitution.

38. What will the man have to do before he can get out of prison? If he does not comply, what will become of him?

What a sobering thought to know that we will not be forgiven by God if we do not do all we can to be forgiven of our sin. If we think we can sweep our anger under the proverbial carpet because the offended person seems to have forgotten it, or they don't seem to be affected by it, we are deceiving ourselves. Just because the injured person can rise above our spiritual immaturity and stupidity, or is too small to defend himself, does not cancel out our responsibility of owning up to our sin.

God does not look down from heaven and think our outbursts are cute, He takes our behavior very seriously. Jesus is giving us fair warning that our angry behavior and sin does not go unnoticed, nor go unpunished by God.

It is human nature to be angry. Anger is an emotion that we can't avoid, but we can control what we do while we are angry. The wonderful news in this lesson is that Jesus has shown us the way to forgiveness for ourselves and for the ones we have hurt along the way. What a true blessing it is to be forgiven for our angry outbursts, and for the possibilities of a restored relationship with those we have hurt.

Let me encourage you to rely on God for the strength it will take for you to go and be reconciled with your brother or sister in the Lord, or your child, spouse, parent, neighbor co-worker, or friend.

Begin each day by asking God to help you control your anger while remembering the words of Jesus.

> *"But I tell you that anyone who is angry with his brother will be subject to judgment. . .".*
> *Matthew 5:22*

Notes

꧁ Prayer ꧂ Part One   Lesson Nine

"I say to you: Ask and it will be given to you." –Luke 11:9

Every now and again, the thought pops into my mind and I wonder how many people around the world might be praying at any one moment (especially on a Sunday!). The ability to hear and answer each person at once is a modern-day miracle. We have a God who can hear billions of prayers at the same time. And what an incredible blessing it is to speak directly to our Creator. Think about it, our Holy Heavenly Father listens to each and every word we speak to Him. What a marvelous wonder it is when you really stop and think about it!

In ancient times God's people communicated with Him on a very formal and ceremonial basis, often through the priests and through a veil in the temple. But Jesus changed all of that when He died. The temple curtain, which separated God from man, was torn in two, symbolizing man's new freedom and access to our Heavenly Father through the blood of Jesus. What an honor, joy, and privilege His sacrifice brought into the lives of the early Christians and all believers to this day!

Sadly, today nearly 2,000 years have passed since the death and resurrection of Jesus, and too many of us have taken this privilege for granted. We've forgotten what an enormous honor it is to enter the throne room of heaven and speak directly with our Creator and Father. If we are honest, many of us would have to admit we would get more excited about being face to face with a movie star or sports hero than we are in going before Almighty God Himself.

When Jesus left the presence of God and came to earth, He continued to communicate with God through prayer. As is so well recorded for us, we know He spoke to God at every defining moment in His life: His baptism (Luke 3:21), the choosing of the twelve apostles (Luke 6:12), and the transfiguration (Luke 9:28). He also prayed at a wedding, a funeral, and before He ate. Jesus prayed early in the morning, late into the night, alone, with individuals and in groups. Jesus stayed close to God by communicating through prayer. It was indeed, His lifeline to His Father.

Prayer is a Christian's lifeline to the Father as well. It is not only our means of speaking to God, but it is His way of speaking to us, answering us, feeding us and sustaining us. If our prayer life becomes disconnected, and we fail to speak to God on a regular basis and only reconnect with Him when we are in a bind, we are not only missing out on one of the most wonderful spiritual gifts offered a believer, but we are squeezing out any chance we might have for a relationship with the Father.

When Jesus Speaks, Will You Listen?

In today's lesson, we are going to learn how to use our sweet God given lifeline to build a solid, effective prayer life. One of the keys to having an effective power-packed prayer life is knowing God's will, and we do this by building a relationship with Him.

For an Effective Prayer Life One Must: Have A Relationship With God

READ: Luke 11:1-4

1. Describe what prayer is to you. Be very detailed.

2. What prompted the disciples to ask Jesus how to pray? *Luke 11:1*

Jesus was more than happy to teach His disciples to pray. Keep in mind as you study this prayer of Jesus that the average Jewish person had very little experience in praying on his own in personal and intimate terms.

The first thing we notice in this model prayer is the beautiful, endearing name Jesus uses to address God. Speaking to the disciples in Aramaic, Jesus does not refer to God as "God" but rather as "Abba" or "Father." This term is an informal, familiar and intimate word, one that children would use for their dads. Jewish slaves were not allowed to use "abba" in addressing their masters; it was too intimate a term. We do not have an equivalent term in the English language that depicts the true connotation of abba/father. The closest word we have is "daddy."

Because the book of Luke is written in Greek, the translation of the Greek word "Father" is used in this passage in place of "Abba" the Aramaic word Jesus used. Later, in other passages in the New Testament, the Aramaic word "Abba" is literally substituted in the Greek manuscript. In each of these Scriptures we are reminded of the intimate nature of the term "Abba" (Aramaic) or "Father" (Greek). It denotes a new, more personal relationship one has with God.

Jesus is instituting a brand new way in which a believer may dare address the Almighty God. Not only is it a new name by which to address God, but He also introduces a new relationship with God available to believers as their Heavenly Father or Heavenly Abba.

But, before we delve into the prayer of Jesus, let's first look closely at these three verses in the New Testament that use the word "Abba," the Aramaic word Jesus used in His model prayer.

3. Who is calling God or instructed to call God "Abba" in these three passages?

Mark 14:36

Romans 8:15

Galatians 4:6

In retrospect, through reading these three passages, one can see that Jesus' followers did indeed come to understand and embrace their new relationship with God. They had no trouble calling God "Father."

In the Old Testament, the Hebrews called God by words that described Him. There are many names for God in the Hebrew language such as Jehovah Rohi: the Lord is my Shepherd (Psalm 23:1); Elohim: God alone is Creator (Genesis 1:1); El Shaddai: God Almighty (Genesis 28:3); and Adonai: Lord Ownership (Psalm 8:1). Until the time of Christ, only formal and descriptive names were used for Jehovah God. But Jesus is revealing a new attitude in which God's children can relate to Him. He is no longer only the God of peace, but rather our Father who gives us peace. And it is only through Jesus' blood that we have this honor.

4. Read Hebrews 10:19-23. What did Jesus do to make Himself our High Priest?

5. What does Peter tell us determines whether our prayers are heard? *1 Peter 3:12*

A key element in building a relationship with our Father is obedience. Have you ever tried to maintain a relationship with someone who contradicts you, second guesses you, and always has to be right? Those bad attitudes rub God the same way! They will keep one's relationship with Him cold and ineffective. It is impossible to build a relationship and a meaningful prayer life with God when one will only obey Him if He does what they tell Him to do, or what they want Him to do. Bossy, one-way conversations will not build a rapport with God.

One of the richest blessings and phenomenons bestowed on a believer is that God desperately desires to have a close relationship with us. He created us for this very purpose. His desire to capture our heart comes from His genuine love for us. As an illustration of this love, let's look at three parables Jesus told in order to demonstrate the lengths to which God will go to maintain a relationship with His children.

> **6. Note who has lost something in each of these parables. What is lost? Then describe what each person does to find that which is lost.**
>
> *Luke 15:3-7*
>
> *Luke 15:8-10*
>
> *Luke 15:11-20*
>
> **7. How does God do the same for the lost today?**

In these three parables, we see God searching hills and dales for lost sheep, looking until He finds them. We see him crawling on His hands and knees, searching in every nook and cranny for His valuable lost treasure. And what does God do when He finds us? As He did with His erring son, He runs to meet us with His arms wide open in welcome!

It is the desire of God's heart to have a relationship with you and me. But the responsibility rests on us to take Him up on the offer or not. To have a powerful prayer life, we must *want* a relationship with our "Abba." We cannot talk about powerful prayers until we are fully committed to having a relationship with God. And proof of our desire is found in our obedience. When we truly understand how very loved we are by God and how deeply He desires a genuine relationship with us, getting to know Him and obeying Him will be our heart's desire.

> **8. In Ephesians 3:14-19 what is Paul's prayer for the church in Ephesus? Is it as important today for us to grasp this truth? Explain.**

When we realize how deeply we are personally loved by God, there will be no stopping the communication with Him. However, if we think God doesn't care, that He let us down in the past or that He does not hear us, we are unable to build the kind of relationship with Him that will build us up and give us the strength, comfort, peace, joy, and wisdom we so desperately desire. Instead our prayers will be ineffective, lacking power or comfort.

9. Why is a relationship with God imperative to having an effective prayer life?

For an Effective Prayer Life One Must: Please God

Another key element in developing an effective prayer life is a desire to please God. If we want a relationship with God, we must have a genuine desire to obey and please Him. It is much easier for God to communicate with us when we come to Him wanting to know what He wants us to do, not telling Him what we want Him to do. He is overjoyed to work with us beside Him. It is then that He can work through us. But He is powerless and impotent when we determine His answers to be null and void if they do not match our expectations. He can only work through the prayers of those who know Him, obey Him, and want more than anything else to please Him. If our hearts are opposed to His will, God cannot speak to us, or work through us.

10. What does John tell us we must do if we are to receive what we ask of God?
1 John 3:21-22

11. What does John tell us we must do so that God can even hear our prayers? *1 John 5:14-15*

Prayer that pleases God—that is in accordance with His will—comes from a faithful and loving relationship with Him.

For an Effective Prayer Life One Must: Know the Will of God

Knowing the will of God is also crucial in sustaining a meaningful prayer life. If we are seeking God's will when we pray, we will receive what we are praying for. But if we are seeking our own will to be done . . . well, God just cannot work with that kind of prayer.

When Jesus Speaks, Will You Listen?

This is not to say God will always say yes to our requests. But He will always answer if our prayer is in accordance with His will. "How do I know God's will?" you might ask. This is a good question. Let's look at this subject for a moment because it is paramount to our prayer life.

READ: Romans 12:2

12. What does Paul instruct us not to do in this passage?

13. What can we do once we stop thinking like the world?

14. List the adjectives from this verse that describe God's will.

Paul tells us to stop thinking like people in the world! Worldly people don't know God and don't understand spiritual things which is why a child of God must think independently of the world. Political correctness is far, far away from the Word and will of God. One must be able to pull their mind out of the world and not be influenced by its philosophy and reasoning. Paul challenges us to have a restored mind, one that can recognize truth even when it is presented through worldly propagating lies. Believers must know how to filter out the world's responses to dilemmas when those responses are contrary to the Word of God. When we can do that, we are ready to know God's will and to accept His answer, regardless of what it might be. But this takes a deliberate effort on our part not to get sucked into agreeing with the politically correct world we live in today, and to stand for the Word of God no matter who or which side disagrees with us.

God's will is always in agreement with His Word. Therefore, it is imperative we know God's Word. The way to a strong relationship with God, one that recognizes His will, is getting to know Him through study. Sorry girls, there are no shortcuts. Prayer, meditation and studying God's Word are the only means of knowing God, His will and what pleases Him.

When we desire God's will over our own, we realize and accept the fact that He does not always say yes, but that He does always do what is best, even when we disagree!

15. Did God always tell Jesus yes? Explain your answer. *Mark 14:35-36*

16. If you pray for your child to be safe in his travels, and he has an accident and is badly hurt, what do you surmise? Did God hear you? Did He answer you? Explain.

One very important lesson we learn from Jesus as he prays in the garden is that we must always pray for God's will to be done, even if it means our own desires are overridden. And we must be genuine about it. Jesus certainly meant for God to do the right thing as He prayed in the garden, even if it meant His own demise.

When we pray, our deepest desire should be for God to do what is best for us or the one for whom we are praying. However, there are times when we just cannot be objective enough to see God's will clearly. I remember when my father was dying of cancer, it was so hard, truly impossible for me at first, to pray for God's will to be done because I so wanted my father to live. Eventually, when my father did not get well, I realized I was working against God's will. It was at this point that I was able to change my prayer and ask God to accomplish His will for my dad, and not mine.

When we pray as Jesus did in the garden, putting God's will over our own desires, we can pray with confidence and with full assurance that whatever we pray for will be done. The answer may be yes or it may be no. But He answers us and gives us what we want when what we want is for His will to be done. Each and every prayer we utter is answered when we give God the leeway to be God.

17. Name times or situations in which it can be difficult to determine God's will. Explain why you think so.

To know God's will, one must know what the Bible says on a subject such as gossip, lying, anger, forgiveness, same sex marriages, or abortion. But what do we do when the dilemma is regarding personal circumstances, specific situations not mentioned in the Bible, such as: Should I make this move? Change jobs? Marry? Start a family? To know God's will in these types of dilemmas, we must pray and ask God to reveal His will through open doors, shut windows or wise Christian counsel. At other times, we need to know His will so we can know how to handle an array of circumstances, such as how to answer someone's Biblical questions, whether to ignore or confront a co-worker's injustice, how to respond to a friend's indiscretions, or how to conquer a bad habit.

No matter what we are struggling with, we can rest assured it is God's desire that we respond correctly. When we pray about these personal matters, He reveals His will in many ways. We might read an article in a Christian magazine about it, a friend may bring it up in conversation, a sermon may be preached on the subject or it may be found in the words of hymn or song. Sometimes just being silent as we pray gives God the opportunity to bring a Scripture to mind or even a concrete action we should take so we can solve our problem. God will find a way to get an answer to us if we are genuinely seeking His will.

18. Name several different ways in which God has brought an answer to your prayers in the past.

We sometimes know intellectually that God listens to every prayer, but too often we begin to doubt He heard us when we don't get our desired answer. We would prefer to believe God is ignoring us than to accept a no.

19. Re-read 1 John 3:22; 5:14-15. In your opinion what are the two most important phrases in these passages?

20. What is the key to knowing one's prayers are heard according to Mark 11:23-24? Give an example of a doubt-filled prayer request.

Have you ever prayed for the rain to stop, opened your eyes, see the storm and say to yourself, "I knew He wouldn't do it." These types of prayers show a complete lack of faith and give God no freedom to do what is best. They are empty words spoken to a god in which we have no confidence. Just imagine after praying in the garden, Jesus becoming angry with God when He heard the footsteps of the soldiers coming and saying to Himself, "I knew He wouldn't do it!" How ludicrous that would have been! Yet, is it not just as ludicrous for us to think like that? We must have the same attitude as Jesus, possessing full assurance that God heard and is acting on our request. It is not enough for us to allow God's will to be done, we must desire His will to override our own.

Our hearts are revealed when we proclaim, "God answered my prayer!" as if surprised. Or we dejectedly moan, "My prayer was not answered," because God's answer was no. I promise you God answers every prayer! A no or wait is an answer! What spoiled children we are to think God is not answering if He doesn't give us exactly what we want, when we want it! What would we think of a child who had a hissy fit every time his parent told him no or to wait? Likewise, it is unimaginable to think of Jesus leaving the garden that night, frustrated because God did not answer His prayer! He left knowing God's answer . . . No, My dear, sweet Son, no.

As we pray, we must not doubt that He hears us or that He will act on every word we utter. Our prayers must be heartfelt; we must mean for God to do something about every single syllable that comes off our tongues. There is no place for flippancy or doubt when we talk to our Father. We know our faith is increasing when, without worry or fret, we accept no for an answer.

Now, with these things in mind, let's get back to the prayer of Jesus.

READ: Luke 11:2

21. What does the word hallowed mean?

The word holy completely sums up who God is. Jesus so brilliantly communicates the complexity with which we ought to address our Father. God is our intimate Father, but He is also a holy and almighty God.

22. What kingdom is Jesus speaking of in Luke 11:2?

The Kingdom of God is a multifaceted subject. But we can all agree on the fact that Jesus wants us to pray for the rule of God to come and for His will to reign in that kingdom. At present, God's will is being carried out through His church and through the lives of believers. As Christians, we should be grateful for the hope we share, the hope of enjoying a heavenly kingdom when our earthly lives are over.

READ Luke 11:3

23. What does Jesus teach is appropriate to pray for? Why is it appropriate?

24. What point did Jesus stress regarding food in Matthew 6:31-33? Does praying for food constitute worry? Explain.

Jesus makes it clear that you and I are within our rights to ask for something we need. But girlfriend, if we pray to God, and then worry about it, it is just wrong. There is no other way to state it. So, what can we do if we find ourselves worrying about something after we have placed it in the capable hands of God?

25. What is Paul's admonishment regarding anxiety? What will God do for those who follow this model? *Philippians 4:6-7*

Paul is very plain in telling us to mix our requests to God with things for which we are thankful. We are to let God know when we are hungry, but at the same time we must never lose sight of the glory and wonder of God. It is He who can feed us daily. In reality, He gives us much more than just daily food. He gives us peace—wonderful, soothing, calming peace during our droughts, financial difficulties or family crises. No amount of food, as lovely as it is, can compare to a life of peace and contentment.

God is always ready to do as we ask. But at times, our prayers just don't seem to be getting through. Every answer seems to be no. Daily food is scarce. What could be the problem? Let's look at some biblical examples of things that hinder one's personal prayer life and are sure to get a no or a deaf ear from God.

26. Why were Jesus' prayers heard by God? *Hebrews 5:7-8*

Even Jesus in His incarnate form understood this primary basic fact: God is the Almighty One. He needed to give up His rights and desires and surrender to God's will. Hmmmm, if it was important for Jesus to be reverent, submissive and obedient, what about you and me?

27. According to these passages, what can hinder ones prayers and result in no when petitioning God? Give examples.

Psalms 66:18

Proverbs 28:9

James 1:6-7

James 4:2

James 4:3

1 Peter 3:12

28. What can take away a Christian's confidence in prayer according to John? Explain how this can happen. *1 John 3:21-22*

Most of the time we are the main obstacle in the way of our prayers being heard and answered by God. We often blame God for not listening or caring, but the truth is He hears every prayer of the righteous and He answers every one of them.

There are so many examples of the Israelites in peril after peril because they were not right with God when they prayed and asked for His help. They were disobedient which brought sin into the camp. It is the same with us today. If we are not getting a yes from God, we must examine our heart and ask: Do I really expect God to step in? Am I trying too hard to do this on my own? Do I have selfish motives? Is there sin in my life?

29. In Mark 11:22-24 what does Jesus tell us we can do if we believe? What is He also saying about those who doubt and do not expect God to do what they ask?

John tells us God listens and answers prayers that are spoken confidently and according to His will (1 John 5:14). If you doubt God will move your mountain and are not praying in confidence, your words are empty and ineffective. God does not hear them.

30. What does James say one who doubts should expect of God in James 1:6-7? What does that say to your heart?

31. What types of situations keep one from asking for God's help or waiting too long to ask?

32. What example does James give of praying with wrong motives in James 4:3? Give examples of what one might pray for today with wrong motives.

God provides daily the things we need and ask of Him—when we ask properly. We should never think we are self-sufficient, well-supplied or that we do not need God's daily provisions. Jesus is pointing out the necessity of humbly expressing our daily needs and concerns, and then fully depending on the Lord to provide them, rather than thinking we produced them ourselves. This response is like that of the drowning man who prayed for God to help him, and when a helicopter came around, he yelled to God, "Never mind, I got my own help." We must depend on God for everything and acknowledge Him in every answer.

READ: Luke 11:4

33. What attribute does Jesus point out is vital to one's relationship with God in these passages?

Luke 11:4

Matthew 6:14-15

Mark 11:25

Jesus knew how important it would be for us to be forgiven by God. He gave His life to make that a possibility for us. He is teaching us to pray daily for our own forgiveness and for our willingness to extend the same mercy and forgiveness to others.

READ: Luke 11:4

34. What is Jesus' last request of God in His model prayer?

35. What do Jesus and His brother James tell us about God and temptation?

Matthew 26:41

James 1:13-14

Every Christian has been tempted by Satan and sadly has succumbed to his evil schemes. Satan's plan begins with just a simple thought in our minds which grows as we delight in it. Eventually, we carry out the ugly act of sin.

> **36. Describe God's part in temptation.** *1 Corinthians 10:13*

Having experienced temptation Himself, Jesus points out our need to constantly be in communication with God regarding our temptations. Knowing how very weak we humans are, Jesus teaches us to pray for God to help us avoid succumbing to the pressure of temptation. What a tremendous relief to know we are not alone in our weakest moments, but that God is there during our temptations, providing the way for our great escape.

> **37. Think of a time you were tempted to sin. What was the mode or way of escape God provided for you?**

Now we are going to take a break to "think on these things," again. Next, we will continue this passage in Luke 11 and examine a parable Jesus told that will help us develop a more faith-based, power-packed prayer life, one that is capable of moving mountains and stopping the rain.

Joseph M. Scriven surely knew the power of prayer when he penned the words to "What a Friend We Have in Jesus." I'd like to end this lesson with the words of this song on the following page.

What a Friend We Have in Jesus

What a friend we have in Jesus, all our sins and griefs to bear;
What a privilege to carry everything to God in prayer.
O what peace we often forfeit, O what needless pain we bear,
All because we do not carry everything to God in prayer.

Have we trials and temptations? Is there trouble anywhere?
We should never be discouraged, take it to the Lord in prayer.
Can we find a friend so faithful, who will all our sorrows share?
Jesus knows our every weakness: Take it to the Lord in prayer.

Are we weak and heavy laden, cumbered with a load of care?
Precious Savior, still our refuge, take it to the Lord in prayer.
Do thy friends despise, forsake thee? Take it to the Lord in prayer.
In His arms He'll take and shield thee thou wilt find a solace there.

Prayer ~ Part Two   Lesson Ten

"I say to you: Ask and it will be given to you." –Luke 11:9

In our last lesson we looked at a model prayer Jesus taught in answer to a request from His followers. They wanted Him to teach them to pray as John the Baptist taught his followers. Christians reverently refer to this prayer as "The Lord's Prayer." We studied how the effectiveness of our prayers is dependent on whether or not we have a personal relationship with God—one that trusts Him implicitly. Peter summed it up well by explaining that God's ears are attentive to those who are righteous but against those who do evil (1 Peter 3:12). With these things in mind, we will concentrate on what we can do to make certain our prayers are heard and answered.

After Jesus taught His followers how to pray and what to pray for, He continued His instructions on prayer by getting into some very specific and practical ways of making prayer a more personal, confident and heartfelt communication with God.

READ: Luke 11:5-13

Jesus told this parable in order to demonstrate just how personal and intimate our relationship with God can be. We find more parables in Luke's account than in any other Gospel book. Very often recording them by using examples of bad behavior to emphasize a positive principle. In this parable Jesus masterfully engages his audience, pulling them into the story with His opening statement: "Suppose one of you has a friend . . ."

READ: Luke 11: 5-6

1. Describe the dilemma in which the friend finds himself.

2. What time is it and what specifically does the friend want from his neighbor?

In Jesus' day people would often travel at night to avoid the heat of the day. Hospitality was an obligation of Jewish families to extend to family members or even strangers. We know Abraham unknowingly

When Jesus Speaks, Will You Listen?

entertained visiting angels, and Job defended himself before his friends by declaring that he had never let a traveler sleep in the streets, but that his door was always open. Mary and Martha were exemplary hostesses, entertaining Jesus and the apostles on many occasions. Jesus condemned Simon for not extending Him the common courtesy of washing His feet when He entered his house.

The host was expected to receive, feed, lodge and protect any traveler who showed up at the door seeking lodging or a meal. It was believed to be a sacred duty. The stranger was treated as a guest, and when he departed, he did so as a friend.

In this story, the traveler arrived at his friend's house late at night which meant his friend's food for the day was probably already gone. Hearing the knock at the door and seeing the weary man must have caused a little panic in the friend. Conscious of his obligations, he invited the weary traveler in and began thinking of ways he could feed the poor guy. Having no food to offer, he quickly remembered a man in his village who would most likely have some food. With dogs barking, he walked next door and woke up his neighbor to ask for three loaves of bread.

READ: Luke 11:7-8

> 3. What two excuses did the neighbor give the friend for not getting up right then?
>
> 4. What prompted the neighbor to get up? Explain why this tactic worked.

In a village home it was very common for the whole family to live in a one-room house, often having one bed for the whole family. Others would have the children and slaves sleep on mats on the floor. This man's family was comfortably tucked in bed and dreaming sweet dreams. Notice the neighbor is not objecting to the request for food; he apparently has plenty, but he just does not want to get up and disturb the kids. So he waits, hoping the persistent friend will think he has gone back to sleep. But the desperate man knocks all the louder. Behind the bolted door, the neighbor wishes the man would give up and go find food elsewhere. But the friend knocks again and again, requesting food each time. Finally, the man realizes his persistent friend will not go away until he gets what he came for. The neighbor reasons, "The sooner I get up and give him some food, the sooner he will go away and stop bothering me and my family."

> 5. Look up the word "boldness" and list some synonyms for it.

6. What aspect of prayer is Jesus demonstrating with the persistence of this man in need of food?

Have you ever told a child he or she could not have something because you believed they were not ready for it? Maybe they were not mature enough, responsible enough, or maybe you just knew they would not appreciate it at the time. God does the same to us. He sees into our hearts and knows if we are spiritually ready to handle what we are asking for.

If we go to God with a request that God does not think we are ready for, He will tell us no. When that happens, what do we do? Do we obediently accept His answer, or do we seek alternative solutions? Persistence in prayer demonstrates to God our acknowledgment that He alone is able to answer our prayer, and that we are depending on Him for the right answer, no matter what it is.

Jesus is not teaching that if we keep begging, God will change His mind. He is teaching that just as the neighbor gave the man what he asked for after he realized the man was not going to go elsewhere for his request, God too is looking for us to rely on Him. At times, God waits for us to truly depend on Him. He allows us to exhaust all our worldly efforts knowing we will eventually turn to Him. At other times, He knows we need to wait a little bit in order to appreciate the blessing adequately. Unlike God, the neighbor had bad motives when finally giving the man some bread. Jesus clearly points out that if a bad-hearted person will grant a request out of annoyance, how much more will a loving Father give to those who ask!

7. Has God ever had you wait on a request you made of Him? Explain.

Tepid, impatient prayers, and those made with fingers crossed and a rabbit's foot in our pockets are going to get a wait-just-a-minute-young-lady response from God. My husband, family and I were privileged to serve in Kenya as missionaries for five short years. While there we worked with many new converts. Some needed to be persuaded to give up their charms and tribal rituals and fully rely on God to heal a loved one or grant their request. They were content to pray and rely on God until they were faced with a grim trial or difficult situation in their life. Then out came the charms.

When Jesus Speaks, Will You Listen?

Aren't we all happy to pray and bring our requests to God until things are out of our control and He doesn't react quickly enough? Then we bring out every human solution we can muster. Jesus is saying we must have faith in God alone. He will deliver what we need, when we need it. It is essential that we stay focused on God in the meantime, faithfully waiting for Him, no matter how long it takes or how many prayers we have to offer. We must trust that God hears our prayers and that He will act upon them when He sees fit. Then we must wait patiently and faithfully on Him. Is it easy to wait when a loved one is suffering, or a spouse is out of a job, or crops are being ruined by rain? No, absolutely not. But the fact remains the same: God will do what is best, whether or not we agree with Him or understand His reasons.

Besides being persistent, our prayers should be specific and in accordance with the will of God. It should always be assumed that God is in control and some things are His alone to decide. Generalities are doubt-filled prayers, prayers we do not expect God to answer such as feed the hungry, heal all the sick, and forgive us all of our sins. Have you ever been in a worship service and heard a prayer for God to forgive us all? Then the next prayer is for the same thing? What happened? Did we all sin between prayers, or did someone pray for something they did not expect God to do?

Some things are known only to God. We must be careful we are not praying for things we know God is not going to do, such as stop all the famines in the world. Where is the faith in that?

On the other hand, if you live in a country that is experiencing a drought or famine, then to pray for God's intervention rain, food and health is a faithful prayer. The difference is one person's prayer does not expect God to act, while the other's does.

When we pray an intercessory prayer, we must realize the person we are praying for has a will of his or her own and that God will not override their will in order to answer our prayer. Be sure you truly expect God to answer your prayer in the way you request. Do not expect drug addicts or alcoholics to simply stop their sinful ways. But do ask God to bring someone into their lives, or to bring about a situation that will bring them back to Him. All the persistence in the world is not going to be effective if our request is too general or if it is against God's will. God is working in that person's life and He already knows what the person needs. He loves that person even more than we do, and He also is actively seeking to save his or her soul.

> **8. Name specific things we might pray for on behalf of another. Then name things we might pray for that are too general for God to answer.**

9. What specifically did Paul pray for in these intercessory prayers?

   Ephesians 1:16-17

   Philippians 1: 19-20

10. Recorded for us are two people who desperately wanted God's intervention. Notice their level of patience as they either did or did not accept God's answer.

    A. How did Sarah respond when God did not act quickly enough for her liking? How did that turn out? *Genesis 16:1, 2, 4-5*

    B. How many times did Paul pray for God to grant his request and how did it turn out? *2 Corinthians 12:7-9*

11. List what happened to David when he patiently waited on the Lord. *Psalms 40:1-2*

Our trust in God is tested when we are not given a yes. Faith that God is doing the right thing by not giving us what we request is what makes our prayers powerful.

Knowing God truly loves each of us should give us the confidence we need to come to Him boldly with our concerns and to be comforted in trusting that our request is in His hands. Doubtful, flippant, impatient prayers are sure to get a negative response and a deaf ear every time.

Jesus continues His story by explaining the degree of persistence with which we must pray in order to get the results we desire from God. Remember persistence confirms dependency.

☕ **READ:** Luke 11:9-10

12. Name the three ways in which Jesus teaches us to be persistent in our prayers. What is the outcome of each?

"So where's the million dollars I prayed for," you might ask. There is an unspoken assumption by Jesus that you are praying with God's will in mind, that you are a righteous person who is seeking the will of God, and that you are not making your request for sheer selfish pleasure.

13. Why does God grant our requests according to 1 John 3:21-22? Why is this true?

14. In 1 Thessalonians 5:17, what is Paul emphasizing and why is it important?

15. List some phrases you use personally in prayers or that you have heard in public prayers that are never meant to be answered, e.g., be with all the widows and orphans.

God is looking for heartfelt words that we truly mean when we ask Him for something or to do something. He is waiting for us to be open to opportunities as we seek answers and truth, and He is waiting to reveal answers to us when we knock. But He can't do that if our prayers are not sincere or if we don't truly believe He is hearing them and answering them. He cannot speak to a deaf ear nor a closed-minded heart.

☕ **READ:** Luke 11:11-12

Just in case this parable did not resonate with Jesus' listeners, He demonstrates His point by comparing the love of an earthly father for his children to God's love for us.

16. What does the son ask for and what would a father never do?

17. How is God like an earthly father? How is He different?

A father who loves his children would never give them something harmful when they are asking for something they need. Yet, Jesus says earthly fathers are capable of evil. They certainly do not possess perfect love. And if earthly fathers, with all their flaws, desire to show love to their children, how much more does our perfect Heavenly Father want to show love to His children?

*READ:* **Luke 11:13**

18. What is the ultimate gift given to us by God? Why is this the ultimate gift?

A full lesson was devoted to the work of the Holy Spirit back in chapter five of this book, but let's briefly look at how He works in our lives through prayer.

19. How does one receive the Spirit?

> **A. How did Jesus receive the Spirit?** *Luke 3:21-22*

> **B. What promise did Jesus make concerning the Holy Spirit?** *Luke 24:49*

> **C. How do we receive the Holy Spirit today?** *Acts 2:33, 38*

The precious gift of the Holy Spirit is given to those who choose to obey and are baptized. Then, the blessings flow endlessly.

> **20. List the things the Spirit does for children of God and note how each will help us in prayer.**
>
> *Ephesians 1:17*
>
> *Ephesians 3:16*
>
> *Romans 8:9*
>
> *Romans 8:11*
>
> *Galatians 5:22-26*

The Holy Spirit plays a crucial part in the daily lives of every Christian. He provides the wisdom we need in making decisions and the power and strength we need to carry out God's will. He fills our lives with every good comfort we can ask of Him: love, joy, peace, patience, kindness, goodness, faithfulness, gentleness and self-control. All these blessings and assurances are given by the Holy Spirit and are ours for the taking, if we only ask.

> **21. How does the Spirit help us when we are weak?** *Romans 8:26*
>
> **22. For what does Paul say God searches and what does God know?** *Romans 8:27*
>
> **23. Why does God listen to the Spirit?** *Romans 8:27*

Have you ever been too sad, overwhelmed, confused, disappointed or hurt to pray? This lonely darkness does not overtake us every day, but occasionally there are times in every person's life when sorrows and circumstances become so overwhelming that we don't even know how to pray. I remember feeling such emotions when our daughter died. I was not angry with God, nor did I doubt Him or want to know why; I was just numb with the sadness and grief of having to live without her. It is in times such as these that the mighty work of the Holy Spirit steps in and speaks to God on our behalf. He speaks to God in groans for which we do not have words. What is He saying? I believe He is explaining our heartaches to the Father, and at the same time is giving us the comfort and peace we need to salve our breaking hearts. He gives us a sense of relief and unexplainable peace by taking our burdens on Himself and voicing them to God for us. What an awesome privilege we have as sons and daughters of God that He would draw us into His presence when we are too weak or broken to go on our own. What a precious gift He has given us.

24. Have you ever felt the relief of the Holy Spirit interceding for you? Explain.

The Holy Spirit is the oil needed for a fine-tuned prayer life. He lets us know when we are not praying according to God's will. He gives us the wisdom we need when we struggle to do the right thing. He supplies the comfort we need in times of stress and sadness when the world has nothing to offer us. He makes sure we have strength and joy when we need it in rough and hard times. How awesome is that?

I want to leave you with this challenge when you pray: Mean every single word you pray and expect God to do every single thing you ask. Will you take the challenge?

If so, in the space below, list some things you might need to work on in your prayer time?

We may need to slow down our thoughts in order to speak what is in our hearts. We may need to think through our motives and desires to be sure we are asking God for something we are confident He will do. We may need to throw out those rote prayers we have been reciting for years. We might need to be more specific in our requests for God to intervene in another's life.

Looking back at the Lord's prayer, we are grateful we are allowed to have such a wonderful relationship with our Heavenly Father. I pray we will work hard to keep that relationship a true one as we keep our prayers specific and real. In the parable, Jesus made us keenly aware of how much God loves each of us and how He longs for us to depend solely on Him.

Best of all, we are given the marvelous gift of the Holy Spirit who aids us in our prayers when we ask, seek and knock according to God's will.

Our prayers will bring about the desire of our hearts when they match the desire of God's heart.

Once again, let the words of Joseph M. Scriven resonate in your heart as you sing, or read the words to "What a Friend We Have in Jesus."

What a Friend We Have in Jesus

What a friend we have in Jesus, all our sins and grief's to bear;
What a privilege to carry everything to God in prayer.
O what peace we often forfeit, O what needless pain we bear,
All because we do not carry everything to God in prayer.

Have we trials and temptations? Is there trouble anywhere?
We should never be discouraged, take it to the Lord in Prayer.
Can we find a friend so faithful, who will all our sorrows share?
Jesus knows our every weakness: Take it to the Lord in prayer.

Are we weak and heavy laden, cumbered with a load of care?
Precious Savior, still our refuge, take it to the Lord in prayer.
Do thy friends despise, forsake thee? Take it to the Lord in prayer.
In His arms He'll take and shield thee, thou wilt find a solace there.

Your challenge:
Keep your prayers real, girlfriend,
keep 'em real.

 Worry   Lesson Eleven

"Therefore I tell you, do not worry about your life …" –Luke 12:22

It must have so pained the heart of Jesus to see how quickly men could turn to worry, even when He, God incarnate was standing right there with them. And I'm afraid things have not changed so much in the following two thousand years. We still tend to worry and mistrust God. We worry about what to do with all our money, or what to do without enough money. Both scenarios can cause one to mistrust God. But God wants us to rely on Him no matter our circumstances. If we're rich and have everything we want, if we're sick with a terminal disease, if we're poor and impoverished, it doesn't matter, God still wants the same thing from all of us, to trust Him with our problems, dilemmas, and trials.

The apostles left everything and followed Jesus. Matthew left a lucrative government job, Simon left a promising position in the military, Peter, Andrew, James, and John left their family fishing businesses. As Jesus looks into the eyes of His apostles and close followers who have legitimate concerns for their families and businesses back home, He teaches this lesson on trusting God and not worrying about worldly things, not even the essentials of life.

In this lesson, we will discover one of the most important aspects of a Christian's life. Jesus is going to show us how to decipher what is important and what is not important in this world. So be prepared to hear some things that may not be easy to accept or put into practice—especially in our culture today. Let's try and open our hearts and minds in order to accept the words of Jesus as He fully intended them to be accepted. Try to not put in a but clause or to rationalize why it is okay for *you* to worry. Some of us have become experts at worrying, without calling it that of course, and therefore freeing ourselves of any guilt.

READ: Luke 12:22-31

1. What did Jesus say not to worry about?

2. Why would the apostles and disciples of Jesus need to be told such a thing?

When Jesus said this, He wasn't just whistling Dixie or merely suggesting they all give it a try, He was very explicit and indeed meant for them *not* to worry.

When Jesus Speaks, Will You Listen?

3. What are things we women tend to worry about? Try to list at least three things.

4. What are we told about working and eating in these passages?

   Ecclesiastes 2:24-5

   Ephesians 4:28

   2 Thessalonians 3:10-11

When Jesus says not to worry, He is not giving us permission to sit around and do nothing while we wait on God to provide for us. God provides our jobs and we are to use those resources to provide for our families. Jesus' point was, whatever our circumstances, we must trust God to provide for our needs.

There are more important things in life than bank accounts, material possessions and retirement plans. **There are even more important things in life than what this earthly life can provide.**

5. Do you agree or disagree with the statement in bold? Why or why not?

The most basic need of man in Jesus' day was food and clothes—survival. It still is today in third world countries. But in the Western World, somehow we have pampered ourselves into more complex basic needs like a running car, or preferably two running cars; money enough for essentials like cable TV, cell phones, dinner out, packaged or frozen everything; a TV, or two, or three; disposable diapers . . . You get the idea. Our basic needs today would dazzle the contemporaries of Jesus' day. But even so, His lesson is still needed for the same basic reasons today. We want what we want, and we are scared without it. Some of us even worry that we may *someday* have to live without it. So we work longer and harder hours at work, which can bring about a whole different set of problems altogether.

READ: Luke 12:23

6. What does Jesus mean when He says that your life and body are more than food and clothes?

7. What do you think is more important than food and clothes?

8. What was Jesus warning against in Luke 12:15? Why?

9. What do you think Jesus would say a man's life consists of?

10. What would Jesus say to the person who has talked himself or herself into believing he or she must work overtime and weekends in order to buy things or store up for the future?

When Jesus Speaks, Will You Listen?

It is not wrong to plan for the future. A retirement is a prudent thing to have, but when we obsess over it to the point we give up church functions and involvement in ministries in order to get ahead at work, we are no longer trusting in God. Worrying about the future can cripple the work in your local church and diminish your influence at home, not to mention what it does to us physically and emotionally.

There are many Scriptures in the New Testament that cover the subject of loving God and putting one's trust in Him. This is how one is able to defeat worry. Without full, complete, and I am talking about total trust in God, we will always be a slave to worry and only fool ourselves when we think we are walking in full fellowship with Him. We cannot neglect being active in the church and think we are doing all He wants us to do. Jesus expects more of all of us than just attendance.

11. What does Jesus say about trust, love and obedience in these passages?

   Luke 11:28

   John 14:15

12. What blessing is promised to those who love and obey the Lord?

   John 14:23-24

13. What does John say about a person who says they love God but does not do what He commands?

   1 John 2:3-6

14. After reading these passages on trusting God and obeying His commandments, what importance should worries have on our lives? What should be the focal point of our concerns?

Building a relationship with God and following His will should be the driving force in every Christian's life. Everything else in our lives will fall into place when these priorities are in proper order. The time and effort we put into worrying about our problems would be more productive if spent seeking the will of God on the matter.

If we truly love God, we will trust Him in all circumstances. That sounds so simple and we all think we do trust Him, but what about worry? Do you worry about your future? Do you worry about your children? Do you worry about your health or the health of your loved ones? Do you worry about your bills or your job? Prayerful concern for these things is a must, but when we become anxious and obsessed over them to the point we take matters into our own hands by seeking worldly solutions, we are revealing a lack of faith in God. And the really scary thing is we won't see it in ourselves. We believe we are taking care of things, but the truth is, we are taking away God's power to do what He needs to do.

If our Almighty Creator could create the world and everything in it, He can handle any problem in our lives. We all accept that intellectually, but sometimes we have trouble applying it when trials come. When it is my child in trouble, my husband who walked away, my loved one who is sick, my job or my husband's job on the line. All of a sudden the words "don't worry" are out the window. All of a sudden it's okay for *me* to worry. I agree, I should trust God and not worry until I have something to worry about.

When Jesus said not to worry, He didn't mean when things are going well don't worry. He meant when things *are not* going well don't worry.

**READ: Luke 12:24**

15. What does David tell us about ravens in Psalm 147:9?

16. Explain Jesus' logic in verse 24. Do you agree with Him? Why or why not?

17. Does the fact that God takes care of us mean we will always have everything we want? Explain your answer.

When Jesus Speaks, Will You Listen?

18. Can we assume that the things we do not have are things God does not want us to have? Take your time and think this question through before writing down your answer.

19. At what point do our concerns cross the line that Jesus is talking about and become a sinful worry?

If a man and his family are hungry, that man should be concerned. He should do all within his power to feed his family. But he should not do something that would be contrary to the will of God for his life. It doesn't justify working so much overtime that his family suffers, or he misses worship and Bible study, or he is too busy to be involved in a ministry. We need to do what we can to eliminate our problems, but God would NEVER favor us neglecting our spiritual responsibility. Sometimes we need to stop, take a breath, step back and live within our means, thus making time for God.

God is always looking for hands and feet to do His bidding. When one is overly concerned with their own life and situation, God's will for them becomes obscure. Though one is limited in time and resources, they may still be exactly the person God needs to fulfill a job for Him.

20. What does one do that is equivalent to the ravens storing up food in barns?

21. What do we rob God of when we worry about the future?

22. What do we rob the church of when we worry about the future?

23. Are YOU truly more valuable than a bird? In what areas of your life are you as vulnerable as a bird and trusting in God to take care of you?

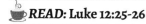READ: Luke 12:25-26

24. Put into your own words what Jesus means in verse 25.

I'm thinking the disciples of Jesus were scratching their heads at this point wondering how to answer the question. If they were honest and told Him what really makes them worry, Jesus would rebuke them. If Jesus said not to worry about food, clothing and stocking up for the future, oh my, what would He make of them worrying about their big problems? No wonder there is not an account of anyone hazarding a guess here.

25. Explain Jesus' logic in verse 26.

26. Personally, how would you answer Jesus' question of why?

In Jack Exum's book "Winning Over Worry," Brother Exum states, "Worry is a prayer to the wrong god." As we worry and fret, we are wasting valuable time and energy that could be used to do the will of God in our life. Worry cannot add an hour to our life nor can it bring us food, only God can do that.

If worrying doesn't bring about results, why do we continue to do it? When you really thinks about it, it does seem ridiculous doesn't it? Worrying about things we can't change zaps us of the energy we need for other things. Our children suffer, our spouses suffer, let's be honest, everyone around us suffers. When we worry we become self-focused and preoccupied with ourselves to the extent we can't see the important things we need to be doing. The things God wants for our lives and the opportunities He puts before us are pushed aside and ignored because we have more important things to think about, to worry about.

> **27. Think about the last time you worried about something. Did it change your situation or help in any way? How could your time have been better spent?**

> **28. And now for the million dollar question, WHY do we worry? What makes us waste our valuable time, energy, and health?**

Worry will never accomplish a single thing. As an anonymous e-mail stated, "Worry is the darkroom in which 'negatives' are developed." As we worry we are actually revealing our unbelief and distrust in God.

 READ: Luke 12:27

> **29. What do Solomon and the lilies of the field have in common?**

If God provides for a pretty defenseless flower . . . hmmm.

 READ: Luke 12:28

> **30. What ultimately happens to flowers and grass?**

> **31. How did Jesus describe those in His audience who worried?**

The fact that Jesus was talking to His closest followers tells us they must have shown some form of anxiety and worry about how they were going to eat, and how they would replace their clothes and pay their bills back home. To some of us, especially the worry warts among us, this may seem like a legitimate thing to worry about. But, look at the rebuke the disciples got. Jesus looked them in the eye, knowing their hardships, and called them men of little faith.

32. If you are a worrier, what would Jesus say to you if He looked you in the eye, knowing your worries and hardships as He does?

READ: Luke 12:29

33. What does Jesus mean by setting your heart?

34. What does Jesus say not to set our hearts on?

35. In our part of the world today, what other things might Jesus include?

36. What are Jesus' final words on the subject of worry in Luke 12:29?

This is where we are going to have to be very honest and see what Jesus is really saying.

Jesus is telling His listeners then, and now, that we are NOT to worry about our problems. Don't do it! He is calling us to trust in God so much that we are willing to take risks by giving God control of our situations to the point we become as vulnerable and dependent on Him as a flower or a bird.

When Jesus Speaks, Will You Listen?

37. What happens to you spiritually when you set your heart on or seek the things you need?

Jesus is so right, whatever our hearts are set on, is what occupies our minds; be that money, retirement, illness, children, or material concerns. When we worry, our self-centered thoughts push out the thoughts of opportunities God is trying to arrange for us. Satan steals the space in our minds needed by God who is trying to get us to think about others and Him. We can't think of both at the same time. It's like trying to talk and listen at the same time. Don't fool yourself, you can't follow God's will for your life and worry at the same time. You must do one or the other.

READ: Luke 12:30

The pagan world consisted of anyone who was not a Jew. These Gentiles fretted over their worries and ran around anxiously trying to solve their problems themselves. Jesus is saying there should be a big difference in the way the pagans solve their food shortage problems, and the way Jews (or Christians) solve theirs.

38. What is the difference in the way a believer and an unbeliever solve their problems?

Unbelievers don't even know God is aware of their needs. They are in darkness and don't have a clue how God takes care of those who love and obey Him. The pitiful thing is there are believers who act like pagans seeking solutions on their own. They do not experience the solutions, blessings, or peace that God is wanting to bestow on them if they would only trust Him.

Sometimes we try and have it both ways. We pray and show our trust in God, but we only pray for things that are not pertinent to our lives; a members' bout with the flu, my neighbor who is grieving, my co-worker's loss of a job. But when it comes to personal things in our lives, we try to handle those ourselves—my job, my retirement, my disease, my children. We trust in God with others' problems, but when something happens to us, whoa, we have a very different reaction. Then we scramble like the world seeking solutions to our problems. We think our problem is too important, too big to give up control, so we keep them to stew over and fret about. As Jesus would say, "Oh, you of *little* faith."

39. What kind of needs do we have that God knows about? Can you think of a need that God knows nothing about or that He has no control of?

Give some careful and deliberate thought to these next two questions. Let your answers be very honest and heartfelt.

40. Are you holding on to any worries, afraid to trust them to God's total control?

41. Is following God's will the most important thing in your life?

READ: Luke 12:31

42. What do we have to do in order to have everything we need?

43. What does seeking the kingdom first have to do with worry?

44. What will be given to the person who does seek the kingdom first?

When we worry about things in this life, it demonstrates a lack of trust in God, a disinterest in the church, and a lack of compassion towards others.

Sometimes we fool ourselves into thinking we are just helping out God, trying to find the solution He wants for us. But the ugly truth is, we are faithless at the moment. We are refusing to leave the outcome of our dilemma up to God to decide. How selfish we are to think that we should never have problems, and that God wants us to be happy. God does not want us to be happy, but rather He wants us to be holy. *Don't worry be happy*, is a myth. Knowing how to give our worries to God builds us up spiritually, and it pleases God to no end.

Jesus expects us to do our best, and to trust God to take care of us however He sees fit. God knows every little thing you're going through, and He has control over everything in your life. That should bring us such relief, comfort and peace.

To close this lesson, let's read some encouraging words from a brother of ours who was writing from a prison in Rome. Paul was not always told yes by God, and by our standards he had lots to be worried about. But He trusted God in every circumstance in which he found himself. It is from a dark, dank and lonely dungeon that Paul penned these words for you and me.

> "Do not be anxious about anything, but in everything by prayer and supplication with thanksgiving let your requests be made known to God. And the peace of God, which surpasses all understanding, will guard your hearts and your minds in Christ Jesus."
> Philippians 4:6-7

> "Therefore I tell you, do not worry about your life . . . ."
> Luke 12:22a

℘Forgiveness℘ Part One — **Lesson Twelve**

"Lord how many times shall I forgive my brother . . . ? I tell you the truth, not seven times, but seventy-seven times." –Mathew 18:21-22

Have you ever had the misfortune of having to truly forgive someone? Someone who hurt you or broke your heart? Maybe it was a spouse, a friend, or a member of the church? If you have, then you know the intense struggle it is to get your heart right and in a place where you can forgive. It is not easy. Forgiveness is not for sissies. But when we do it right, when we do it like Jesus says to do it, it is one of God's most beautiful blessings. Not only are we free of hate and vengefulness, but we are blessed with peace and reconciliation that this world cannot understand or appreciate.

Forgiveness from one's heart does not come naturally. Rather it must be learned, nurtured, trained, and at times, forced. Real forgiveness is a "God thing" in every sense of the word.

In the passage we are about to study, Jesus will explain clearly that there is a difference between true forgiveness and halfhearted or fingers crossed behind one's back, kind of forgiveness.

As we enter this lesson, it is important to understand that Jesus is speaking of forgiving a person who has SINNED against us, not merely hurt our feelings or disappointed us. It is a purposeful sin against you, such as: spousal betrayal, character assassination, dishonoring a promise or trust, robbing, cheating, swindling or going back on a contract. You get the idea.

Let's do a little background work and find out what began this whole discussion between Jesus and His disciples. In the verses that precede this passage, Jesus has introduced the idea of forgiveness, which triggers a thoughtful question by one of His listeners, and will bring us to our lesson today.

READ: Matthew 18:15-17

> **1. Who has sinned against whom in verse 15?**
>
> **2. Explain the steps one is instructed to take in a case like this.**

3. Contrast how our human nature wants to react to a person who has sinned against us to how Jesus is teaching we must react in verses 15-17.

In these verses Jesus is stressing the significance of putting a great effort into trying to get the guilty party to repent. Most of us do not have a heart that naturally wants to forgive someone who has hurt us, and it is out of the question if the guilty person does not apologize with a contrite heart. Some of us even demand some groveling, and still we feel the guilty person needs some cold shoulder time. After all, we don't want to appear as though we condone their bad behavior. The last thing our human hearts want to do to that unrepentant, hurtful person is to gingerly show them the error of their ways in hopes they will want to repent and reconcile.

This idea of actively seeking forgiveness left the disciples baffled. Like many of us, they wondered what happened to the chastising and punishment for the guilty one. This new teaching on forgiveness made no sense to Jesus' followers; they were utterly mystified. In their bewildered state the disciples were left with two choices: to accept the fact that they were not forgiving others as they should, or to pridefully hold tight to their personal way of thinking on the matter.

Now, we come to the passage for our lesson today. And leave it to Peter to be the one to voice concerns about this mysterious procedure of forgiving others as he asks Jesus for clarification.

READ: Matthew 18:21-35

4. What does Peter ask Jesus in verse 21? Reading between the lines, what do you think motivated Peter to ask this question?

The rabbinic law required a person who had been wronged by someone to forgive them a maximum of three times. Peter, knowing this law, thought himself very generous when he asked Jesus if seven times would be enough to forgive someone who had wronged him.

Have you ever felt justified in not forgiving someone? Peter surely must have. Forgiveness can become such a tangled web. Our pride and ego can get in our way of seeing clearly the steps we need to follow. We, like Peter, want a clearly defined rule spelling out for us exactly when we are, and when we are not, obligated to forgive others. Peter wanted to know how many times he had to put up with this evil person who had wronged him. What Peter doesn't understand is that it is never permissible to withhold forgiveness. And, not only that, but the guiltless person is even responsible for making every effort they can to persuade the guilty person to apologize!

To answer Peter's question on how many times one must forgive another, Jesus tells a very outlandish parable.

Again, remember we are not addressing hurt feelings or trivial disappointments, but rather sin against us. This kind of wrongdoing will only occur a handful of times in a person's lifetime.

> **5. In your own words define forgiveness. What is the desired objective of forgiveness?**

Forgiveness was not a virtue in the pagan world. It was seen much as it is in our world today, as a weakness and something to avoid. The tough and strong get even; they don't forgive! And they certainly don't initiate reconciliation when someone else hurt them! But we know God has other ideas concerning forgiveness, ideas that defy our human nature and call us to rise above our worldly urge to retaliate.

> **6. List some reasons why you believe forgiveness is difficult at times.**

To seek revenge is so very human. We are by nature dreadfully vindictive creatures, it's almost frightening how naturally it comes to us at times. Jesus is calling us to control our carnal tendencies regarding striking back, getting even, or wanting to hurt those who hurt us. Instead, we are to encourage their repentance which hopefully will lead to reconciliation.

READ: Matthew 18:22

> **7. Using different Bible versions, what are some variations on the answer Jesus gives Peter regarding how many times to forgive others? Why do you think He exaggerated so?**

8. In Luke 17:4 how many times does Jesus say to forgive others? What is the responsibility of the guilty party in this passage?

9. What is the response of the apostles in Luke 17:5? What do you think is meant by their comment?

As Jesus teaches this lesson in Matthew 18, He is fully aware of the Jewish teaching on the subject of forgiveness. Peter also knows the 3-times-you're-out forgiveness law that Jewish rabbis taught. That is why Peter and the others are so confused. They have always had a clause in the rule book that would allow them to seek revenge. Peter is seeking clarification, wanting to know if he is hearing Jesus right, and if he is, how in the world a person can actually do that. When Peter threw out a number to Jesus he was trying not to underestimate the right answer. Peter suggested seven times, a number he believed was very generous, given it was more than double the Jewish allowance for forgiving another.

10. Whether Jesus meant to forgive 7 times or 490 times, or anything in between, what is the point He is making?

Jesus' response to Peter's question shocked Peter and all those listening. They were expecting Jesus to answer their question using a number between one and three. To forgive a person 490 times, or as we read in Luke, seven times in one day, was unthinkable! Peter must be wondering, who could ever expect anyone to forgive that many times! Can't you just see the disciples looking down at the ground, shaking their heads, exhaling, and whispering, "Increase our faith!" And I'm imagining Peter is still wondering, so, seriously, when is it okay to lower the boom on that sinner and fulfill my right for revenge.

The parable Jesus is about to tell is a hyperbole, told in this exaggerated fashion in order to clear up once and for all what true forgiveness is.

READ: Matthew 18:23-25

11. To what is Jesus comparing this parable? What does this term stand for?

12. Who does the king represent in the parable?

13. What is the king wanting to do in verse 23?

14. How much money does the servant owe the king?

15. What is the servant's punishment for his crime?

16. What is the law for a man who cannot pay his debt? *Exodus 22:3, 2 Kings 4:1*

This servant is in deep, deep trouble. His debt to the king has been discovered.

A lifetime of the servant's wages would not touch this debt. Hebrew law allowed debtors to be sold at auction along with their families to help pay their debts. So this king was perfectly within his rights to have the servant and his family sold.

We have all been in the place of this servant who has sinned and is in dire need of forgiveness. If we translate the word debt to sin in this parable, we understand that every sin we commit against one another is ultimately a sin against God too, as we are breaking His law when we sin. And one day, our Father will call us to give an answer as He did this servant in the parable. With this in mind, let's see how this parable plays out.

When Jesus Speaks, Will You Listen?

READ: Matthew 18:26-27

17. What is the response of the servant? What does he ask of the king?

18. In your opinion, was the servant truly sorry and was his request reasonable? Why or why not?

This guilty servant approached the king in a physically humble position, but instead of humbling his heart and begging for forgiveness, he asked the king for some time so he could gather the money to pay him back. He is caught red-handed and his only reaction was to plead for time so that he could pay back the king and correct this embarrassing situation. How very human of him.

In the Greek numerical system 10,000 was the largest number and a talent was the largest currency sum. Using the two together, Jesus could not have come up with a larger sum of money for the servant to owe the king. In modern language we would say he owed the king a zillion dollars.

To give us a perspective as to how much money 10,000 talents was, it took the average working man over 15 years to make one talent. And the servant suggested he'd pay back 10,000! What a ludicrous notion! This poor guy would never have been able to pay the king back. Which is exactly the point Jesus is making by using this hyperbole.

19. In what ways do we show the same arrogance as the servant when asking God to forgive us?

20. How did the king respond to the servant's request? Why did he respond so?

21. Do you believe the king ever intended for the servant to make good on his promise to pay back the 10,000 talents? Why or why not?

22. What do we learn of repentance in 2 Corinthians 7:10?

If you have ever been forgiven by someone that you have wronged, you know how the servant should have felt when he heard the king say, "You are forgiven your debt to me, you're free to go." The servant did not deserve to be forgiven. Yet, he was shown mercy and grace, not because he was worthy of it, but because the king was kind-hearted and merciful.

God is always ready to forgive those who humble themselves before Him and repent with all their heart, asking for His forgiveness. But He will not forgive those who will not repent. God's holiness will not allow Him to forgive a sinner who will not repent. He loves the person, but He cannot forgive or resume a relationship with that person until he confesses his sin and asks for forgiveness. Forgiveness is a response to something. In the same way you're welcome is a response to thank you. You wouldn't reply you're welcome if someone hadn't first thanked you, unless of course, you were being snide or training a child. It's the same with forgiveness. God cannot forgive someone who has not asked for His forgiveness.

We too can only forgive others if asked (love them yes, but forgive and reconcile, no). That's why it is so important to make every effort to give the guilty person opportunity to ask for forgiveness. The cold shoulder treatment, gossiping to all we know and pridefully daring them to show their face, is not the kind of attempts at making peace that Jesus is talking about. Even if after trying with all your heart to bring the guilty person to repentance, they still refuse, it still does not open the floodgates of permission to not love them. It is never right to hold a grudge while waiting for the guilty person to ask for our forgiveness, nor do we have permission to harbor hatred, hurt others or seek revenge. Love your enemies and do good to them would come into play (Luke 6:27).

READ: Matthew 18:28

23. What is the first thing the servant did after he left the presence of the king?

24. How much did the fellow servant owe the king's servant? Was it possible to pay back this debt?

A denarius was a Roman coin worth one days wage. It took 6,000—10,000 denarii, to equal one talent. This made the king's servant's debt around 500,000 times more than his friends debt to him.

25. Describe in your own words the heart and human thinking of the king's servant as he met his friend on the street.

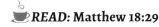READ: Matthew 18:29

26. Write the words of the two servants that are identical to each other. *Matthew 18:26, 29*

27. What is the difference between the attitude and heart of the two servants as they beg for time and patience?

Our Heavenly Father has such an extraordinary capacity to love and forgive His children. As undeserving as we are, God keeps on forgiving us when we sin. Oftentimes the things we are called to forgive each other of pale in comparison to that which God has forgiven each of us.

And who has not been indebted to our Father and in need of His forgiveness? What Jesus is teaching in this parable is if you need to be forgiven by God, you better not withhold forgiveness, carry a grudge or seek revenge against another. Whew, increase our faith Lord!

We must always examine our motives when asking for forgiveness. Are we just sorry for getting caught, or for the sin and all the ugliness associated with it? Is our apology specifically for forgiveness for the harm we caused another, or is it mixed with excuses for our actions, such as, "I'm really sorry for that, BUT you deserved it" or "I never would have done that if you hadn't . . ."? If we are truly seeking forgiveness of others and of God, we must not be arrogant or halfhearted about it. There is no substitute for a genuine, contrite heart. As in the parable, others can detect our rationalizing, and so can God. We are only fooling ourselves when we pretend to be sorry while secretly making excuses for ourselves.

28. What do you learn from these passages on forgiveness and repentance?

   Ephesians 4:32

   Romans 2:4

READ: Matthew 18:30

29. What is it about this ungrateful servant that gets our dander up?

30. In what way do we tend to respond just like him?

What an ungrateful, self-centered man this servant of the king was. How dare he refuse to forgive someone who was offering a fair promise to pay back his debt after being forgiven so much by the king. Then again, don't you believe that these are the same sentiments of our Heavenly Father as He looks down on you and me, seeing us grab one a sister by the throat and cruelly choke her because she dared to sin against us.

31. Read these Scriptures and explain why we must forgive others.

   Matthew 6:14

   Matthew 6:15

   Colossians 3:13

We will all one day be called before our God and King, who will look at our account and judge us using the same measure for forgiveness that we use on each other.

In our next lesson we will look in depth at how we can overcome the human tendency to hold grudges and punish those who sin against us. We will discover how God's way of forgiving frees our souls of guilt and hatred and blesses our lives, as well as the lives of those who have sinned against us.

❧ Forgiveness ❧ Part Two — Lesson Thirteen

"Lord how many times shall I forgive my brother . . . ? I tell you the truth, not seven times, but seventy-seven times." –Mathew 18:21-22

Have you ever wondered as Peter did, how many times you are expected to forgive someone, or if you are even required to forgive them at all if the sin against you is too horrendous. It is human nature to feel justified to hate, seek revenge, or carry a grudge.

As we study the parable of the Unmerciful Servant Jesus told in Matthew 18, we learn of a king who demonstrated great love and compassion on an undeserving servant of his. The servant having owed the king more money than anyone could imagine, begged for time to raise it, offering the king options which were both out of the servants reach and unrealistic.

After ordering the punishment due the servant and his entire family, the servant's begging for time made the king change his mind. Not only did the king do the unimaginable and forgive the whole debt, but he canceled the order for punishment as well.

Then, this dirty, rotten servant walked out of the courthouse, seized an old friend on the courtyard steps and got into a scuffle with the man demanding payment for a few dollars owed him.

This story conjures up so much emotion. We see that the good folks in Jesus' day were enraged at this ungrateful, wicked, and downright cruel servant of the king. It's interesting that we still have the same reaction today as the characters in the parable did nearly 2,000 years ago.

Today we are going to look at our own hearts and see what we can learn from this unmerciful servant. We'll learn how to forgive and be reconciled with others. We will look at how those who have been wronged should respond, as well as how those who need forgiveness should respond. Either way, we have a responsibility to seek reconciliation and forgiveness.

READ: Matthew 18:31

> **1. What did the others who witnessed this injustice do and why?**

When Jesus Speaks, Will You Listen?

Who can read the response of the king's servant and not be enraged? Can Jesus tell a parable or what? He's got everyone on the edge of their seat, including you and me. This man who was forgiven a debt he could never in a zillion years pay back, could not forgive a little puny debt that was easily resolved and cleared up in a couple of days.

READ: Matthew 18:32-33

> **2. What did the king do after he heard about the actions of his ungrateful servant?**
>
> **3. What specifically was the king upset about?**

Oh, what human creatures we are! We delight in the mercy, love and forgiveness our Heavenly Father showers on us. We relish these thoughts, then turn around and refuse to forgive a brother or sister in Christ, or a spouse, a child or a parent who injured us in some way. Though they beg to be forgiven, we withhold it from them. We believe they have not suffered quite long enough and we are determined to punish them in every way possible, and for as long as we deem necessary. If this is you, please consider seriously what Jesus said in Matthew 6:14-15. This is not a suggestion, it is our reality. If we do not forgive others, God will not forgive us. Please don't deceive yourself. Holding a grudge and punishing others, even though they were in the wrong, will keep you from being forgiven by God. The guilty person can be forgiven and exonerated by God, but you, dear one, cannot.

Forgiveness is not always easy. Oh, the small things are easy enough. A slight, being taken for granted, being taken advantage of, or hurt feelings can be aggravating, irritating, and very hurtful. But when a spouse breaks a vow, a friend betrays you, a parent is abusive, or a neighbor or co-worker slanders or cheats you—these things take the help of God to forgive.

Some may say one has a right to hold a grudge and withhold forgiveness in cases such as these. But God is saying no, no, no, you must give up the idea that you ever have the right to hold a grudge or seek revenge. Vengeance is reserved for God, and God alone.

READ: Romans 12:19-20

> **4. List the things Christians are called to do in this passage that, in your opinion, defy human nature.**

Knowing God is watchful and promises to avenge us Himself releases us from the burden of repaying and punishing others. Does this mean it is easy or painless to forgive them? No, absolutely not. It may be the hardest thing you will ever do. But it is God's will for you, it is what He expects of you.

Giving the blessing of forgiveness to someone who has wronged or hurt us brings us an array of blessings in return.

If you are holding a grudge against someone and withholding forgiveness, you are battling a great war. On one side is Satan and all he brings to your life: bitterness, hatred, bad memories anger, hurt, and depression. Satan loves whispering in your ear and reminding you how hurt you are, how undeserving of this pain you are, and how badly the hurtful person needs to learn a lesson. On the other side of the battle ground is a meadow full of sunshine, forgiveness, love, mercy, peace, and a hope of mended lives and restored relationships. Why wallow in the dread and gloom of unforgiveness?

5. List the blessings that come to you and to the one who hurt you when you are able to let go and forgive.

6. List the physical and spiritual destruction that comes to you and to the one who hurt you when you do not forgive them.

If a person asks for your forgiveness everyday, Jesus said you are to forgive them each and every time. These situations can become very complicated and difficult to sort out. Oftentimes the outcome is out of our control; one cannot force another to forgive, neither can one force the guilty one to seek forgiveness. If someone will not forgive or ask for forgiveness, it makes reconciliation and fellowship difficult, or even impossible.

If the guilty one does not ask for forgiveness, Jesus says we are to seek reconciliation with them anyway. We do this in order to bring them back to their relationship with us and ultimately with God. Exceptions to this would be physical abuse or adultery. Not that these acts are unforgivable—because they absolutely are—but, building back the original relationship is not always possible, nor is it always prudent. Still, even in these cases, one must seek forgiveness and a peaceful closure in order to be free of all animosity and hate.

7. You have heard the phrase "forgive and forget." Do you believe that is possible?

8. Is it possible for God to forgive and literally forget?

After one forgives another, is he or she to forget that the hurt and loss ever took place? That sounds nice, but is it really? Does God forgive and literally forget? We read many Scriptures this way, but is that what they really mean? Is it possible for God to forget one's sin? I do not believe it is. He forgives thoroughly, but He cannot forget. For instance, did God after forgiving Adam and Eve, forget they ever sinned? Did He forget that Abraham, Moses, David, or Peter sinned? Does He forget that you and I have slipped and sinned? Let's look into these questions a little more closely.

9. What do these Scriptures say about God's forgiveness?

Psalm 103:12

Romans 4:8

Hebrews 8:12

2 Corinthians 5:9-10

How do we mesh these two thoughts together? God remembers our sins no more, and yet, we will be judged for everything we have done. The problem is in our interpretation of the word remember. Not remembering does not mean God forgets, but rather He chooses not to call our sins to mind or ever hold them against us.

In the same way we cannot forget, nor should we forget, the hurt caused by others. For example, would you forget that your neighbor mistreated your child? If you did you would turn around and subject Junior to the same danger repeatedly. One's memory is important, it keeps him from repeating past mistakes that could set him up to be hurt again.

Once we have forgiven a person, we must choose, as God does, not to call the hurts to mind. One mustn't continually punish the guilty person, or continually dwell on the hurts, holding the event over their head. This is self-destructive and will bring nothing but heartache.

This story by Simeon well illustrates this principle:

"A man strikes me with a sword, and inflicts a wound. Suppose, instead of binding up the wound, I am showing it to everybody, and after it has been bound up I am taking off the bandage constantly, and examining the depths of the wound, and making it fester, is there a person in the world who would not call me a fool? However, such a fool is he who, by dwelling upon little injuries or insults, causes them to agitate and influence his mind. How much better were it to put a bandage on the wound and never look to it again." Simeon
(The Biblical Illustrator Copyright © 2002, 2003, 2006 Ages Inc.) From the Commentary Biblical Illustrator)

READ: Matthew 18:32-33 (Again)

10. What does the king call the slave? What brought on this anger in the king?

11. What do Jesus and his brother James say about mercy in these passages?

   Matthew 5:7

   James 2:13

READ: Matthew 18:34

12. Describe the emotion of the king. What was the new sentence given the servant? How is this punishment different than the first?

When Jesus Speaks, Will You Listen?

13. What were the terms of the sentence? Was it possible to meet them?

This servant could not be in a worse situation. He has burned his bridges with the good-hearted king which was his only hope. His new punishment is endless torture. The king could not tolerate a servant who would not reciprocate the mercy and forgiveness shown him.

Like the king's servant, we all are faced from time to time with the decision to forgive or punish someone who has hurt us, to dwell on the offenses or let them go, to seek revenge or reconciliation. The king's servant chose poorly, and the king took it very seriously.

READ: Matthew 18:35

14. How is God going to treat us if we do not forgive our brother or sister?

Jesus is not fooling around with emotions in this parable. It is a grave warning of the fate of those who do not forgive another from their heart.

15. Explain the difference between forgiving someone and forgiving someone from your heart.

16. How does pride come into play when one is faced with the choice to forgive or not forgive?

How can we know if our forgiveness is genuinely heartfelt or we are merely going through the motions? This takes an open and honest examination of our hearts. Heartfelt, genuine forgiveness does not continue to wish the other ill will. On the other hand, it doesn't mean you must be bosom buddies either, but you must be able to stop the hate and animosity you feel for the person even if he or she does not ask for your forgiveness.

> **17. What does God say about those who repent versus those who do not repent?**
>
> *Romans 2:5*
>
>
> *Acts 3:19*
>
>
> **18. What does Jesus say about our acts of worship if we know there is someone who we have wronged and have not sought reconciliation?** *Matthew 5:23-24*

Witnessing the treatment of the king toward the unforgiving servant in the end gives us a glimpse into how God will deal with us if we refuse to forgive others or to seek forgiveness and reconciliation. To not be forgiven by God is a chilling thought. The Psalmist says in *Psalm 130:4* "But with you there is forgiveness; therefore you are feared." And for those who will not forgive, there is much to fear. As in the parable, the king did not give the servant another chance, the punishment was quick and it was permanent. The time for begging, groveling and forgiving was over. Jesus is not trying to win friends as He brings this parable to a close. He is, however, trying to win souls. If there is someone you have not forgiven, please listen.

> **19. On what basis is one to fear God?** *Psalm 130:2-4*

One last aspect of forgiveness we have not covered yet is that of forgiving one's self. When we are the culprit, how do we let go of the guilt, shame and regret that Satan so happily reminds us of constantly? How do we put it behind us and get on with following and doing God's will in our lives? First, let's establish who has the power to forgive our sin.

20. What lesson was Jesus teaching the Pharisees in Luke 5:24?

21. Put into your own words what these passages have to say about our own sins.

   1 John 1:9

   Romans 8:1-2

If we know in our heart that Jesus has the authority to forgive sin, and that God longs for us to repent and reconcile our relationships with Him and others, then why don't we feel forgiven when we pray? Why do we still feel the shame and guilt that can weigh so heavily on our hearts? Sometimes it is easier to forgive others than it is to forgive ourselves. But think about it, who profits when we stay guilt-ridden, when we constantly beat ourselves up over and over again? Not forgiving ourselves keeps us spiritually paralyzed, unable to move on and become all God has in mind for us to be.

If you have truly repented, and have done everything you can to be reconciled, you are forgiven regardless of how you feel! It makes Satan smile from ear to ear when he can keep us from forgiving ourselves and becoming useful in the kingdom.

22. How can one set his heart at rest when it condemns him and he feels unforgiven?
1 John 3:19-20

When we refuse to forgive ourselves we are demonstrating a lack of faith in Jesus as the one who has authority to forgive every sin. We are also demonstrating a lack of faith in God and His credibility to do what He says He will do with our sin. Carrying guilt in one's heart is not only taking on an undue burden, but worse than that, it is also calling God a liar.

Satan does all he can to keep us from forgiving ourselves. But what Satan whispers in our ear is not the truth. It is just his ploy to keep us in a state of doubt, sorrow and regret, keeping us too preoccupied with chastising ourselves to carry on and do the things God has prepared for us to do. The good news, and this is indeed good news, is that Satan cannot force anyone to believe his lie; he can only try!

23. Explain the schemes of Satan that Paul alludes to in 2 Corinthians 2:10-11?

Forgiveness is not an option. Whether you have sinned against another or someone has sinned against you, we have the same obligation to forgive and seek reconciliation. The penalty for not forgiving is serious, and the punishment, eternal.

I'd like to end this lesson with the wise and comforting words of the prophet, Micah.

"Who is a God like you,
Who pardons sin and forgives the transgression of the remnant of His inheritance?
You do not stay angry forever but delight to show mercy.
You will again have compassion on us;
You will tread our sins underfoot and hurl all our iniquities into the depths of the sea."
Micah 7:18-19

Bibliography

Barclay, William. *The Daily Bible Study Series: Matthew, Mark, Luke, John. Philadelphia.* The Westminster Press, 1975

Barnes, Albert. *Barnes' Notes, PC Study Bible Formatted Electronic Database.* Biblesoft Incorporated, 2006.

The Biblical Illustrator. *PC Study Bible Formatted Electronic Database.* Biblesoft Incorporated, 2006.

Black, Allen. *The College Press NIV Commentary: Mark.* Joplin: College Press Publishing Company, 1995.

Black, Mark C. *The College Press NIV Commentary: Luke.* Joplin: College Press Publishing Company, 1996.

Bryant, Beauford H. and Mark S. Krause. *The College Press NIV Commentary: John.* Joplin: College Press Publishing Company, 1998.

Burge, Gary M. *The NIV Application Commentary: John.* Grand Rapids: Zondervan, 2000.

Chouinard, Larry. *The College Press NIV Commentary: Matthew.* Joplin: College Press Publishing Company, 1997.

Clarke, Adam. *Adam Clarke's Commentary, PC Study Bible Formatted Electronic Database.* Biblesoft Incorporated, 2006.

Cole, R. Alan. *Tyndale New Testament Commentaries: Mark.* Grand Rapids: William B. Eerdmans Publishing Company, 1989.

Exum, Jack. *Winning Over Worry.* Fort Worth: Star Bible Publications,

France, R.T. *Tyndale New Testament Commentaries: Matthew.* Grand Rapids: William B. Eerdmans Publishing Company, 1985.

Henry, Matthew. *Matthew Henry's Commentary on the Whole Bible, PC Study Bible Formatted Electronic Database.* Biblesoft Incorporated, 2006.

Brown, David, Andrew Robert Fausset and Robert Jamieson. *Jamieson, Fausset, and Brown Commentary, PC Study Bible Formatted Electronic Database.* Biblesoft, Incorporated 2006.

Keener, Craig S. Editor. *InterVarsity Press Bible Background Commentary: New Testament.* Westmont: InterVarsity Press, 1993.

Lewis, C.S. *Mere Christianity.* New York: Macmillan Publishing Company, Inc., 1960.

Morris, Leon. *Tyndale New Testament Commentaries: Luke.* Grand Rapids: William B. Eerdmans Publishing Company, 1988.

Tasker, R.V.G. *Tyndale New Testament Commentaries: John.* Grand Rapids: William B. Eerdmans Publishing Company, 1960.

Wiersbe, Warren. *Bible Exposition Commentary.* Colorado Springs: Chariot Victor Publishing, and imprint of Cook Communication Ministries, 1989.

Made in the USA
San Bernardino, CA
19 April 2019